SRA Early Reading TUTOR

Student's Book

Susan L. Gibbs Monica Leigh Campbell Shawnna Helf Nancy Cooke

SRA

Columbus, OH

The McGraw·Hill Companies

MW00483855

sraonline.com

SRA

Printed in the United States of America

Send all inquiries to this address:
SRA/McGraw-Hill
4400 Easton Commons
Columbus, OH 43219

ISBN-13: 978-0-07-605393-3
ISBN-10: 0-07-605393-8

4 5 6 7 8 9 MAL 14 13 12 11 10

The McGraw·Hill Companies

Lesson 1

Letter-Sound Correspondences

s

a

Review: Letter-Sound Correspondences

a

s

Lesson 2

Letter-Sound Correspondences

m

a

s

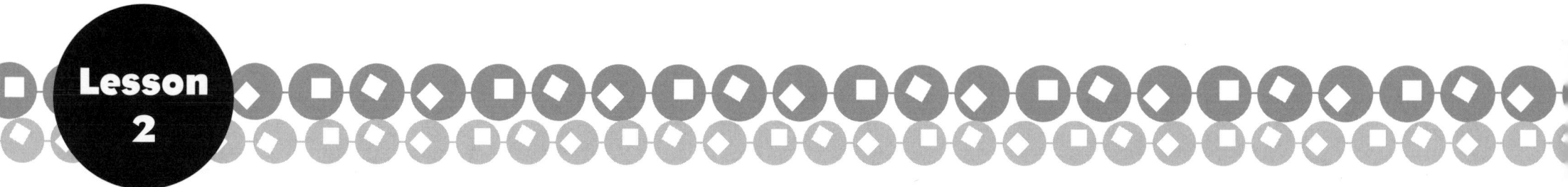

Review: Letter-Sound Correspondences

m

s

a

Lesson 3

Letter-Sound Correspondences

a

s

m

Review: Letter-Sound Correspondences

m

a

s

Lesson 4

Letter-Sound Correspondences

a

s

m

t

Review: Letter-Sound Correspondences

t

s

m

a

Letter-Sound Correspondences

m

s

t

a

Lessons 1-5

Mastery Test

Letter-Sound Correspondences

m

s

a

t

Lesson 6

Blending Sounds into Words

sat

Letter-Sound Correspondences

t r

s

m a

Lesson 6

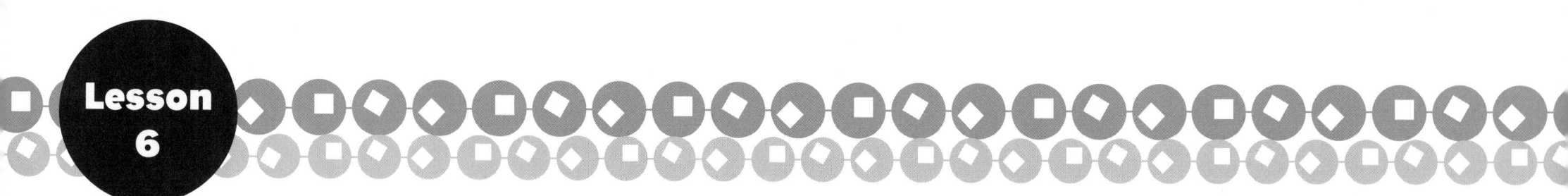

Review: Letter-Sound Correspondences

m

s

r

t

a

Review: Blending Sounds into Words

sat

Lesson 7

Blending Sounds into Words

mat

Letter-Sound Correspondences

r t

s a

m

Lesson 7

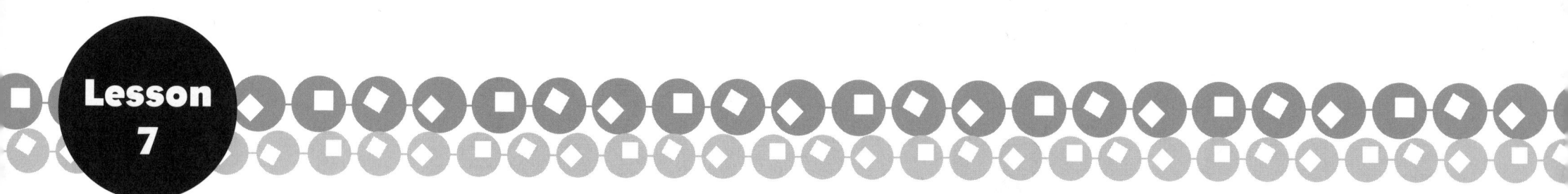

Review: Letter-Sound Correspondences

t

m

a

s

r

Review: Blending Sounds into Words

sat

Lesson 8

Blending Sounds into Words

rat

Letter-Sound Correspondences

r

m

i

s

t

a

Lesson 8

Review: Letter-Sound Correspondences

a m

s

i

r t

Review: Blending Sounds into Words

at

Lesson 9

Blending Sounds into Words

sat

Letter-Sound Correspondences

f a

s t

r

m i

Lesson 9

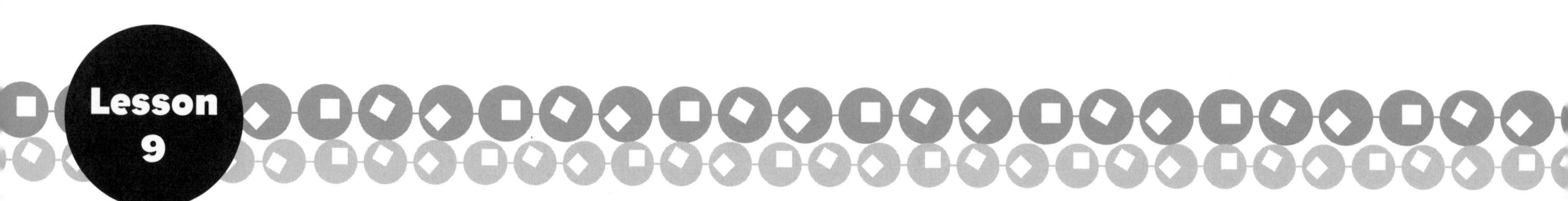

Review: Letter-Sound Correspondences

t f

r

s

i

a

m

Review: Blending Sounds into Words

am

Blending Sounds into Words

ram

Letter-Sound Correspondences

f i

t a

m

s r

Lessons 6–10

Mastery Test

Letter-Sound Correspondences

i a

t

f

r

s

m

Blending Sounds into Words

fit

rat

Lesson 1[illegible]

Letter-Sound Correspondences

a m

i d

s

r f

Lesson 11

Blending Sounds into Words

rim sat mat

Lesson 11

Review: Letter-Sound Correspondences

d

s a

m

f

Review: Blending Sounds into Words

rim

Lesson 12

Letter-Sound Correspondences

d a

i t

r s

f m

Lesson 12

Blending Sounds into Words

fat mitt Sam

Lesson 12

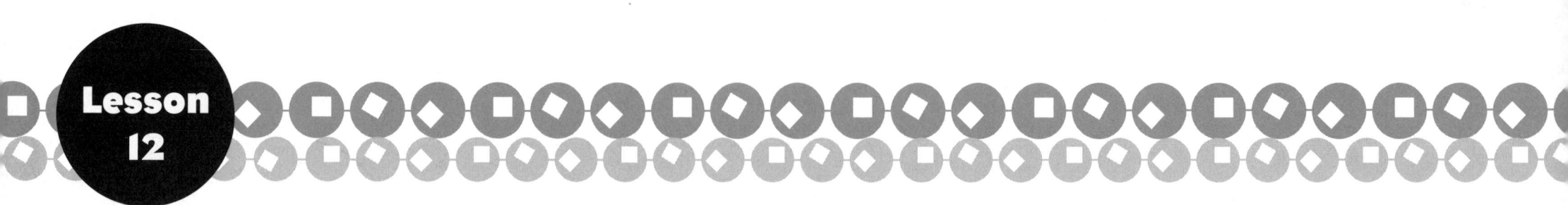

Review: Letter-Sound Correspondences

i

d

a

r

t

Review: Blending Sounds into Words

Sam

Letter-Sound Correspondences

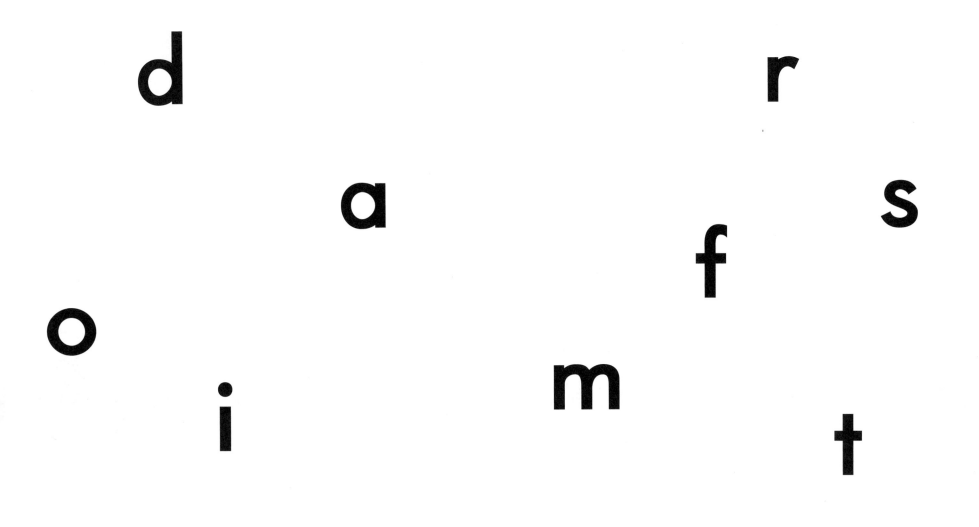

d r

a s

f

o

i m

t

Lesson 13

Blending Sounds into Words

fit rid dim

Lesson 13

Review: Letter-Sound Correspondences

m

d

f

r

a

Review: Blending Sounds into Words

Sam

Lesson 14

Letter-Sound Correspondences

m t

s i

a

r o

f d

Blending Sounds into Words

fit

rid

dim

Review: Letter-Sound Correspondences

m o

t

r d

Review: Blending Sounds into Words

Sam

Lesson 15

Letter-Sound Correspondences

s t f

g o

m

a d i

Blending Sounds into Words

it is fat

Lessons 11-15

Mastery Test

Letter-Sound Correspondences

f a

t o

i m

d

Blending Sounds into Words

mad

fit

Lesson 16

Letter-Sound Correspondences

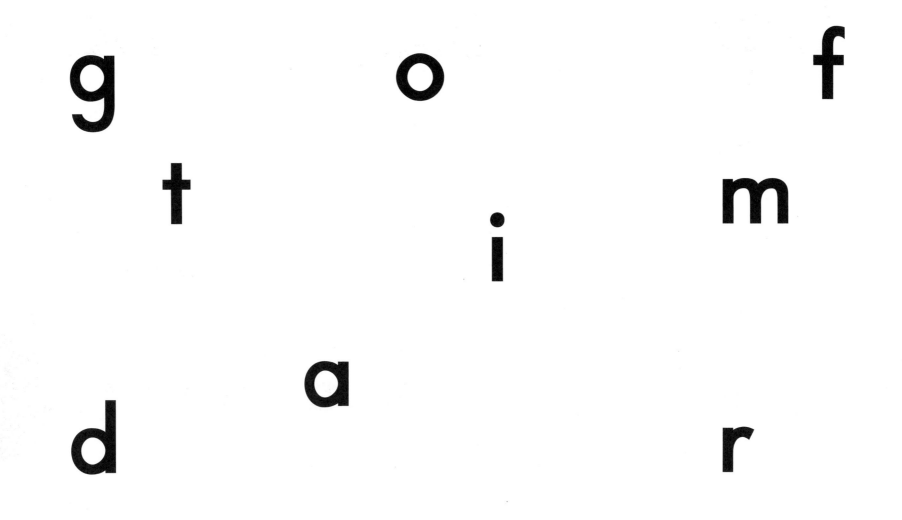

g o f

t m

i

a

d r

Lesson 16

Blending Sounds into Words

dog rat dig

Lesson 16

Review: Letter-Sound Correspondences

g t

r m

i

Review: Blending Sounds into Words

rot

Lesson 17

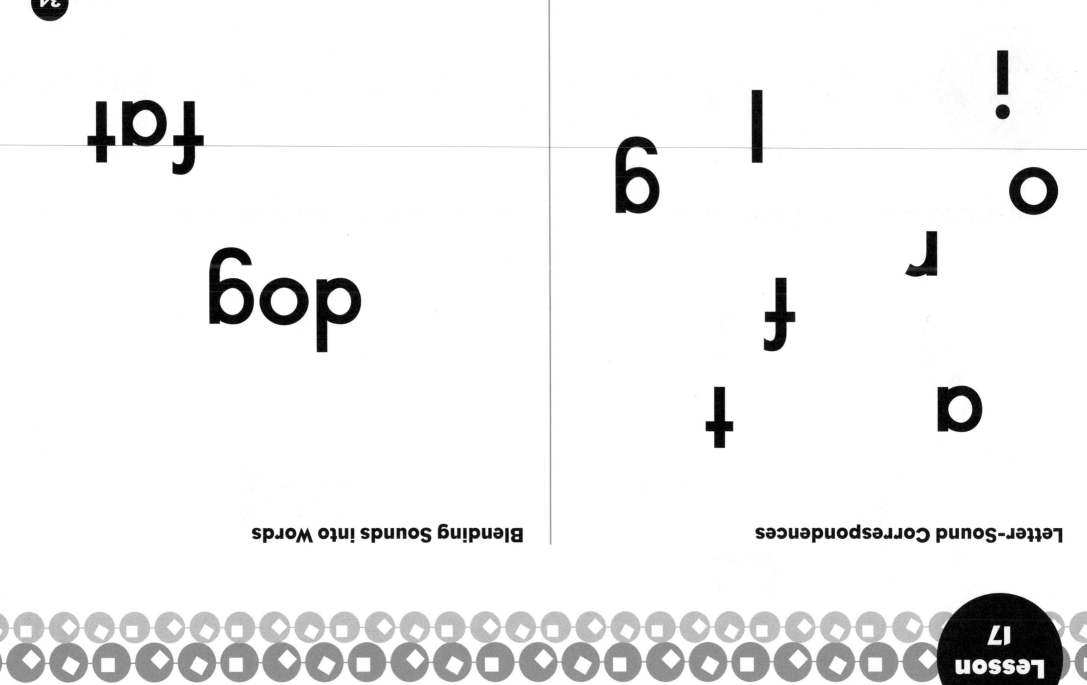

Letter-Sound Correspondences

a t

f

r

o g

l

i

Blending Sounds into Words

dog

fat

Review: Letter-Sound Correspondences

l g

f

i d

Review: Blending Sounds into Words

dot

Lesson 18

Letter-Sound Correspondences

l ā o

a i

g t

f r

Lesson 18

Blending Sounds into Words

it dog is

Lesson 18

Review: Letter-Sound Correspondences

g

l

o

f

Review: Blending Sounds into Words

lot

Letter-Sound Correspondences

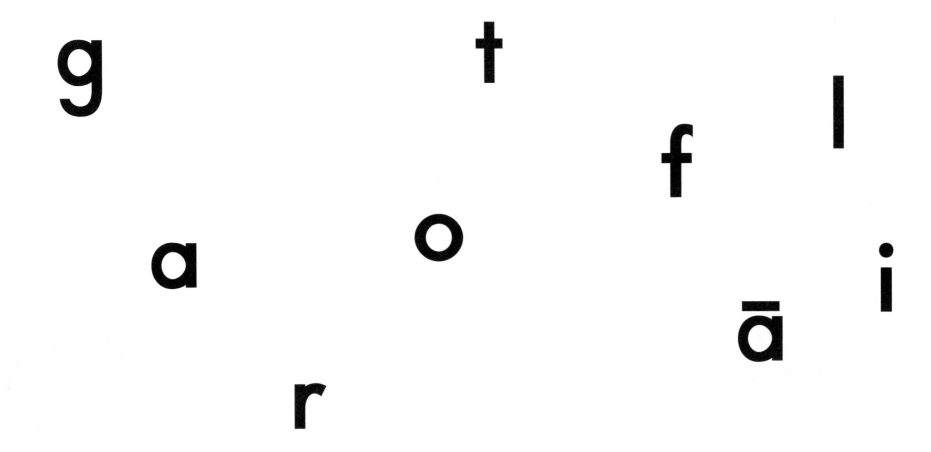

g

t

l

f

o

a

i

ā

r

Lesson 19

Blending Sounds into Words

is fat it

Lesson 19

Review: Letter-Sound Correspondences

r

i

o

l

t

Review: Blending Sounds into Words

it

fat

Lesson 20

Letter-Sound Correspondences

ā g

s

o

a

l i

m

r h

Lesson 20

Blending Sounds into Words

fat it dig

Lessons 16–20

Mastery Test

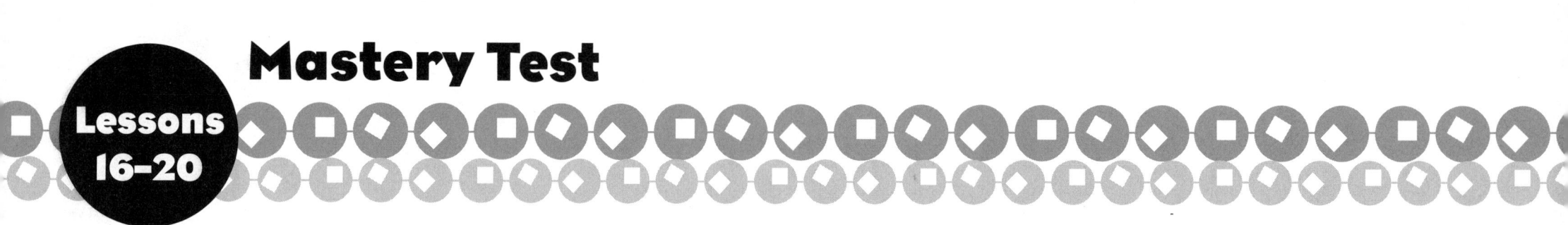

Letter-Sound Correspondences

o

d

m

a

l

g

i

Blending Sounds into Words

log

did

Lesson 21

Letter-Sound Correspondences

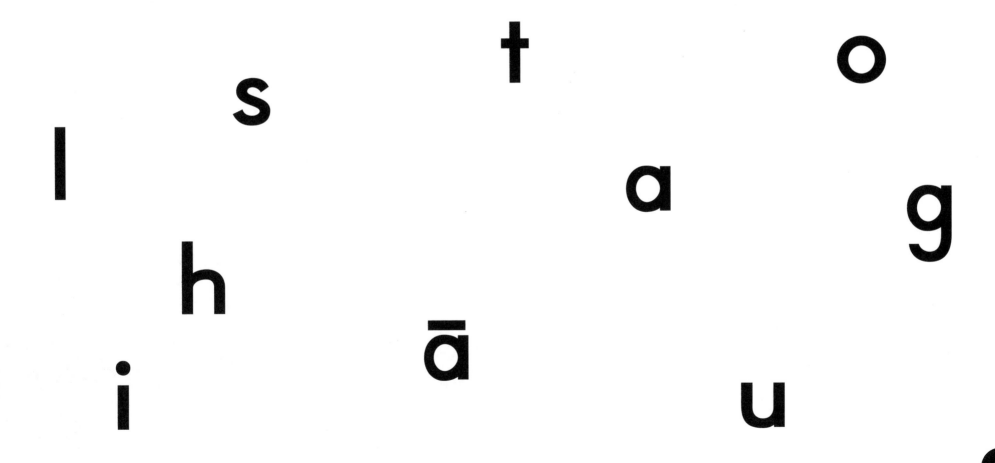

t o

s

l

a

g

h

ā

i

u

Lesson 21

Blending Sounds into Words

sad ā dog

Review: Letter-Sound Correspondences

u i ā

h g

a l

t

o s

Review: Blending Sounds into Words

sad

Lesson 22

Letter-Sound Correspondences

m g s a

t i

u h l

c ā

Lesson 22

Blending Sounds into Words

ā Sam hog

Lesson 22

Review: Letter-Sound Correspondences

t o u

h i

a g l

s ā

Review: Blending Sounds into Words

hog

Lesson 23

Letter-Sound Correspondences

g

h

t

i

b

u

m

s

Blending Sounds into Words

his   him   it

Lesson 23

Review: Letter-Sound Correspondences

u s

m g

i

t h

Review: Blending Sounds into Words

gum

Lesson 24

Letter-Sound Correspondences

s t

u

c

g

i

b

n

Lesson 24

Blending Sounds into Words

big

mat

his

fist

fit

bat

Lesson 24

Review: Letter-Sound Correspondences

n b

t i

h

g s

Review: Blending Sounds into Words

rug

Lesson 25

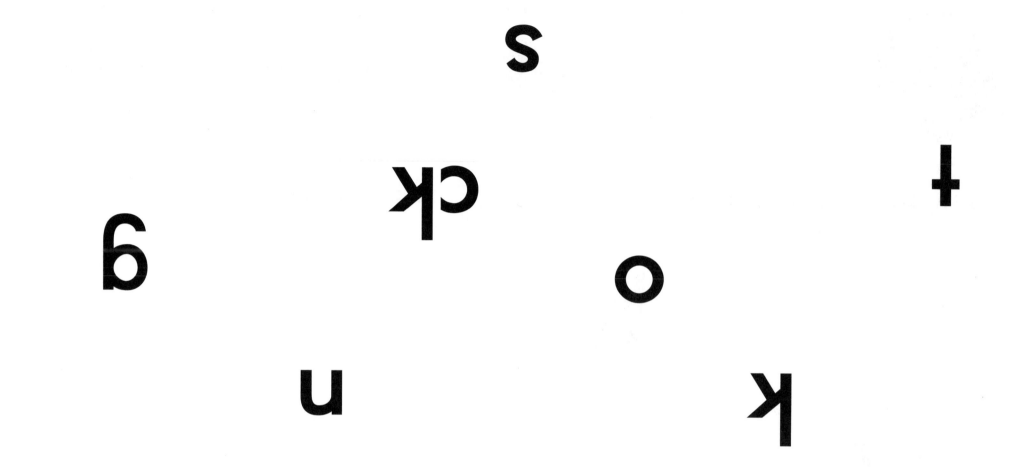

Letter-Sound Correspondences

k

n

o

g

t

ck

s

Blending Sounds into Words

sack

sun

got

sit

not

Lessons 21-25

Mastery Test

Letter-Sound Correspondences

r o

i l

m g

u

Mastery Test

Blending Sounds into Words

him sun not

Lesson 26

Letter-Sound Correspondences

e n u

i a

b

l o m

s

ā g

Lesson 26

Blending Sounds into Words

big

it

can

run

dog

fast

Lesson 26

Blending Sounds into Words

it is big.

it can run.

it is ā dog.

Lesson 26

Review: Letter-Sound Correspondences

k

n

e

b

l

Review: Blending Sounds into Words

let

Lesson 27

Letter-Sound Correspondences

a l

s g o i

b u

n e ā

w

Blending Sounds into Words

tack

will

fit

on

it

rug

Lesson 27

Blending Sounds into Words

it is ā tack.
it will fit on ā rug.

Review: Letter-Sound Correspondences

e

b

k

n

l

Review: Blending Sounds into Words

let

Lesson 28

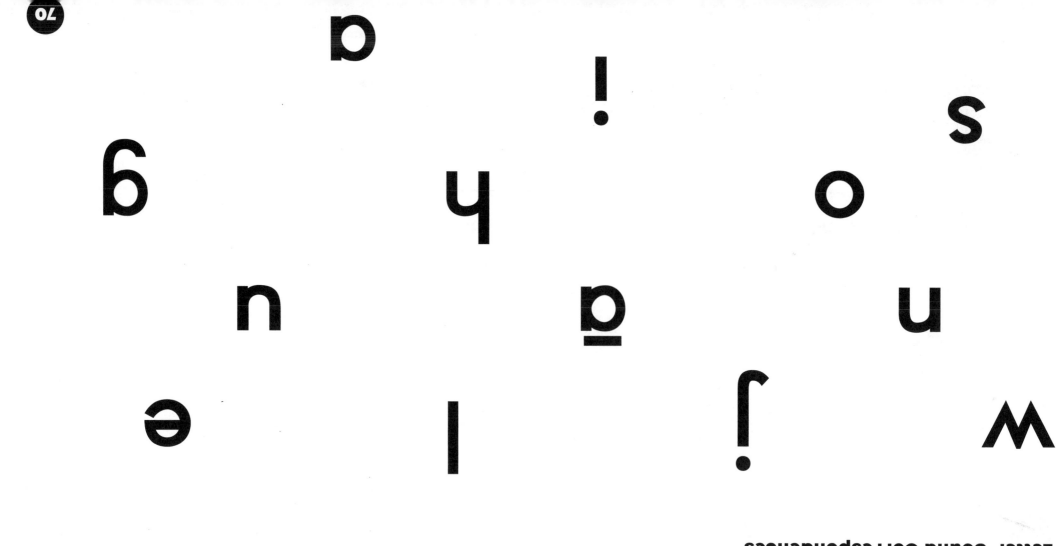

Letter-Sound Correspondences

w j l e

n ā u

o h g

s i

a

Blending Sounds into Words

rock

on

hot

log

ā

has

it

Lesson 28

Blending Sounds into Words

it is ā hot rock.

it is on ā hot log.

Lesson 28

Review: Letter-Sound Correspondences

w n

j b

e

k

l

s r

m

Review: Blending Sounds into Words

big

Lesson 29

Letter-Sound Correspondences

p w j c

e n

u h o s a

i ā l

Lesson 29

Blending Sounds into Words

log hot ā

can it

jump run

fast off

Lesson 29

Blending Sounds into Words

it can jump off ā

hot log.

it can run fast.

Review: Letter-Sound Correspondences

n p w

l

j

a

b

k

e

i

r s m

Review: Blending Sounds into Words

hot

Lesson 30

Letter-Sound Correspondences

a l ā

i s o

h u y

e

c n

j w p

Lesson 30

Blending Sounds into Words

red

pot

not

can

tin

pan

Lesson 30

Blending Sounds into Words

is it ā pot?

is it ā pan?

is it ā can?

Blending Sounds into Words

it is not ā pot.

it is not ā pan.

it is ā red can.

it is ā tin can.

Lessons 26–30

Mastery Test

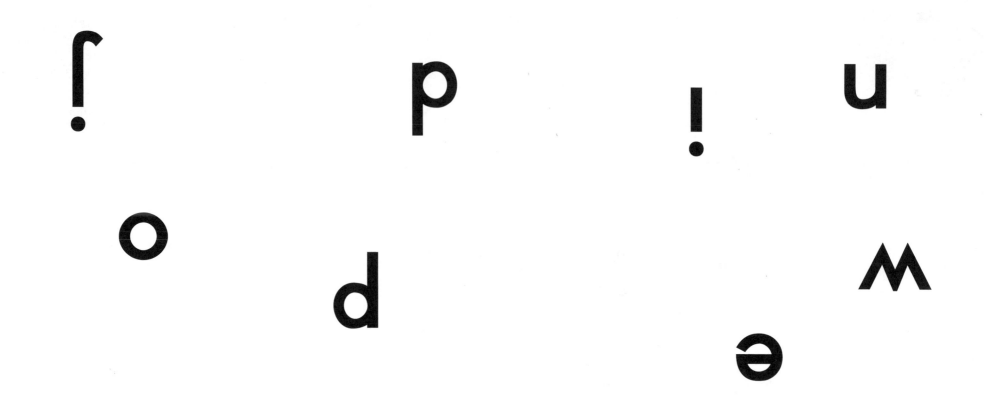

Letter-Sound Correspondences

e

w

p

o

i

n

d

j

Mastery Test

Lessons 26–30

Blending Sounds into Words

pop nod lip

Lesson 31

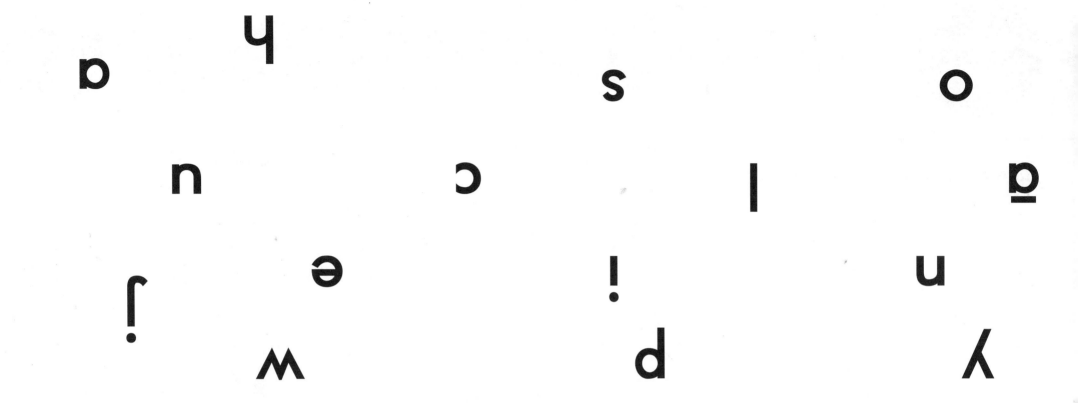

Letter-Sound Correspondences

y p w

n i e j

ā l c u

o s a

h

Blending Sounds into Words

yet

beg

can

net

pet

fast

run

jump

yam

ā

Lesson 31

Blending Sounds into Words

ā pet can beg.

can ā pet jump yet?

ā pet can jump and beg.

Review: Letter-Sound Correspondences

a

p

y

w

b

k

e

s

ā

l

Review: Blending Sounds into Words

set

Lesson 32

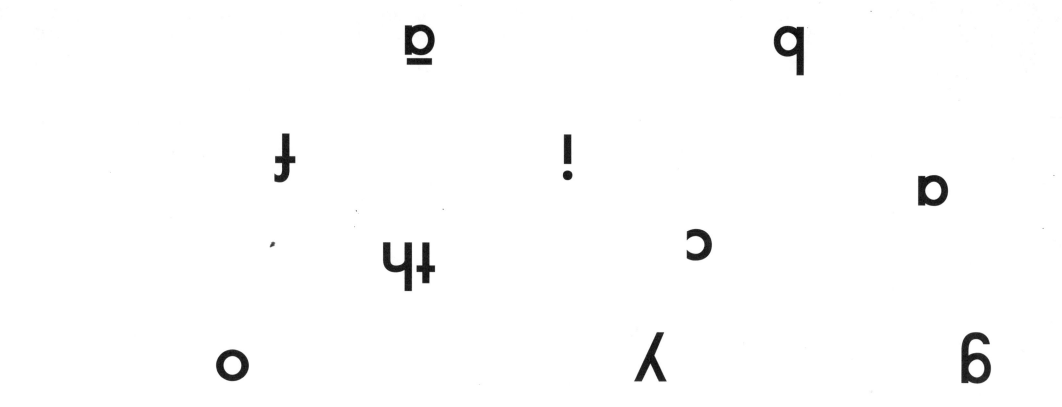

Letter-Sound Correspondences

g y o

c th

a i f

b ā

Blending Sounds into Words

is

it

mē

cat

yet

fast

sēē

big

Lesson 32

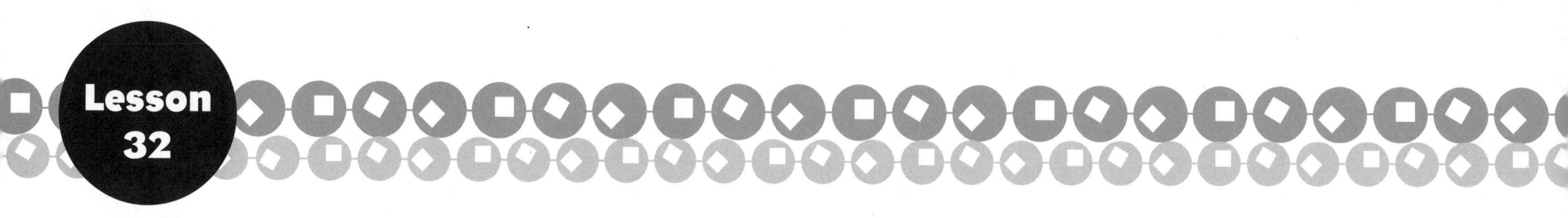

Blending Sounds into Words

it is ā big rat.

ā rat can run and run.

it can run fast.

Review: Letter-Sound Correspondences

th i

n ā

y

o a

Review: Blending Sounds into Words

yet

Lesson 33

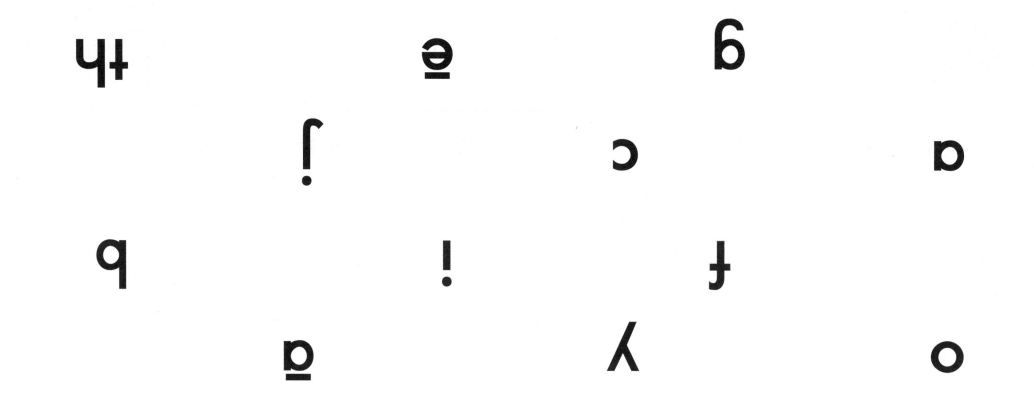

Letter-Sound Correspondences

o y ā

f i b

a c j

g ē th

Blending Sounds into Words

cat

sēē

yet

big

it

mē

fast

Lesson 33

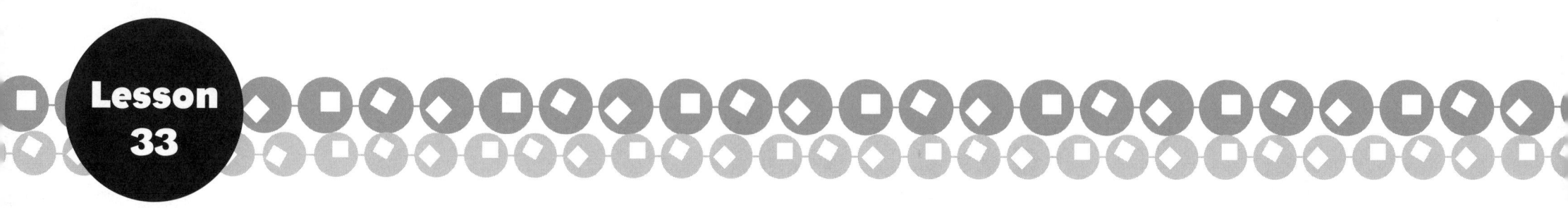

Blending Sounds into Words

it is ā big rat.

ā rat can run and run.

it can run fast.

Lesson 33

Review: Letter-Sound Correspondences

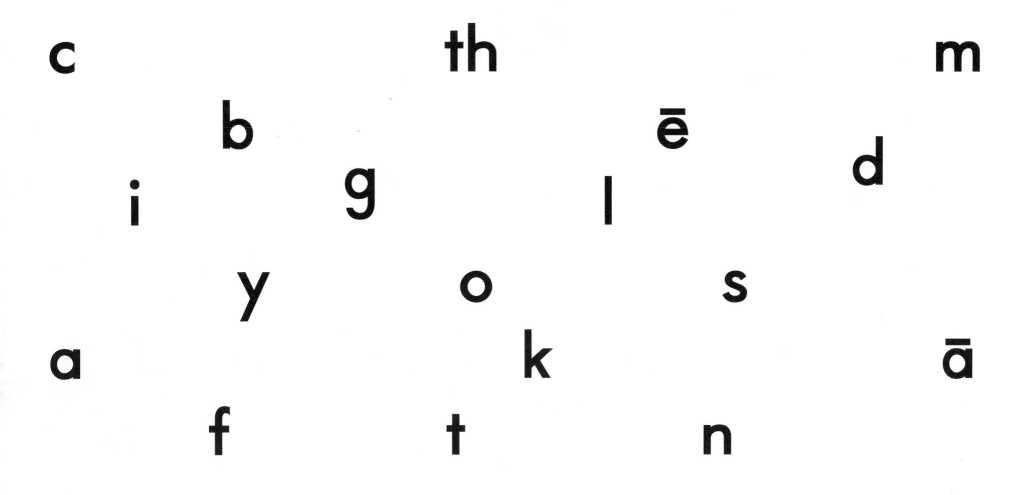

c th m

b ē

d

i g l

y o s

a k ā

f t n

Lesson 33

Review: Blending Sounds into Words

yet

Letter-Sound Correspondences

I r g

y s th

o ā b ī

ē a

Lesson 34

Blending Sounds into Words

thē

not

this

mē

ā

red

sēē

Blending Sounds into Words

this is ā red dog.
it is not ā big dog.
it is not ā hot dog.

Lesson 34

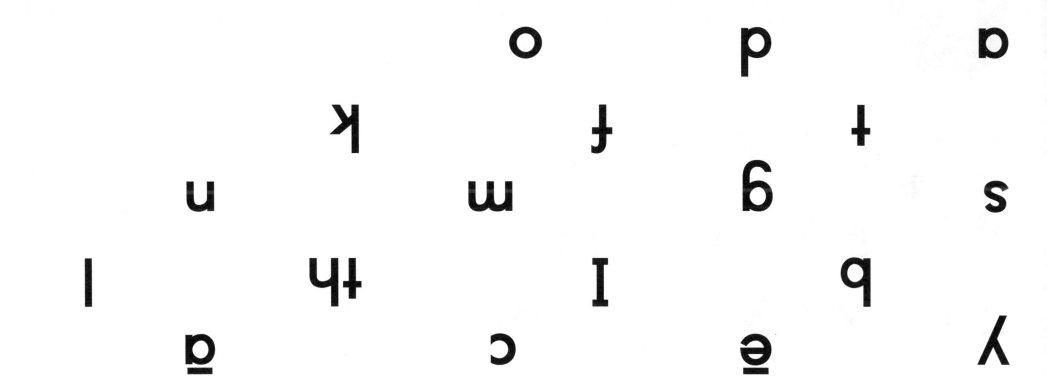

Review: Letter-Sound Correspondences

y ē c ā

b I th l

s g m n

t f k

a d o

Lesson 34

Review: Blending Sounds into Words

sēē

Lesson 35

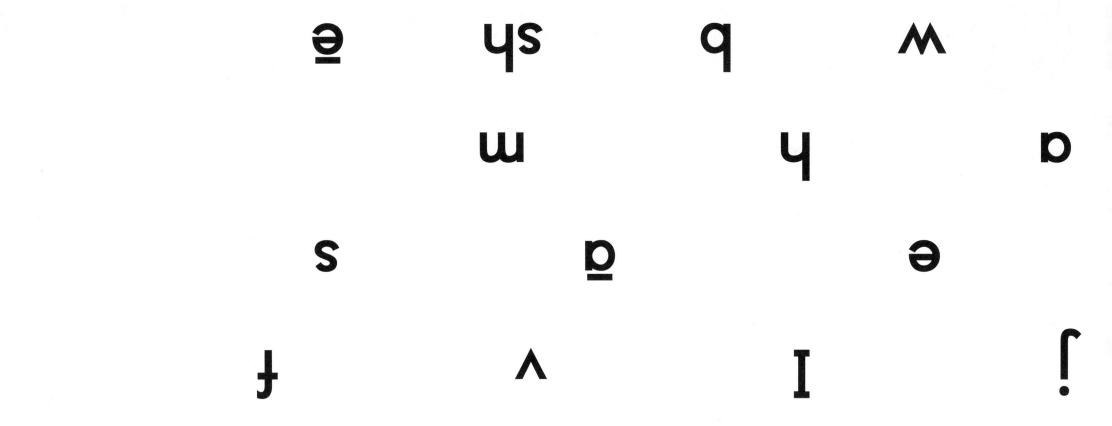

Letter-Sound Correspondences

j I v f

e ā s

a h m

w b sh ē

Blending Sounds into Words

jet ā this

if

fast sēē

thē

Lesson 35

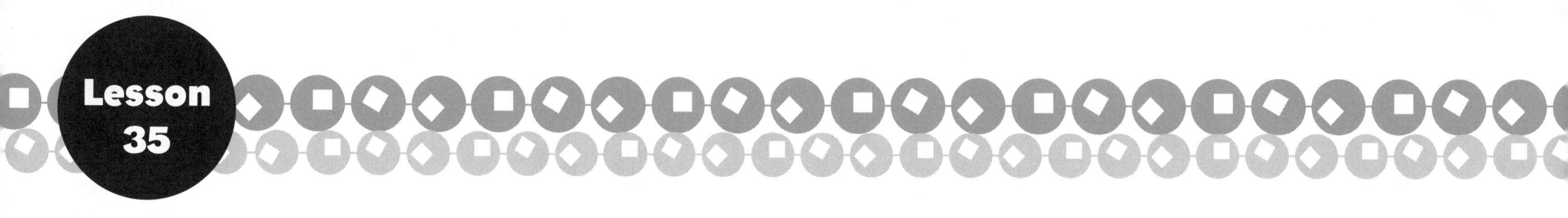

Blending Sounds into Words

I sēē ā jet.
it is ā big jet.
thē jet is red.

Mastery Test

Lessons 31–35

Letter-Sound Correspondences

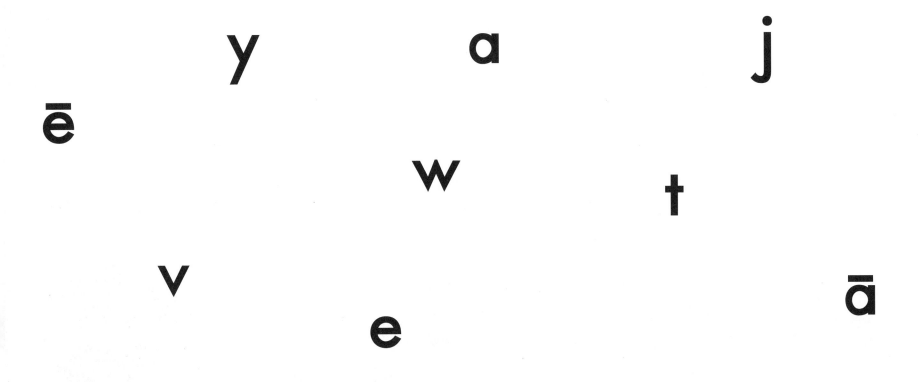

y a j

ē

w t

v ā

e

Mastery Test

Lessons 31-35

Blending Sounds into Words

jet   sēē   wē

Letter-Sound Correspondences

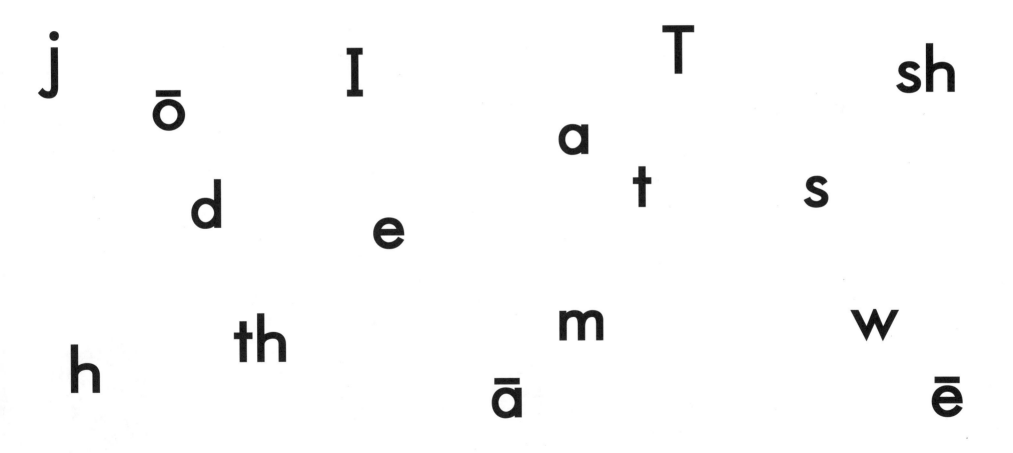

j ō I T sh

a

d e t s

h th m w

ā ē

Lesson 36

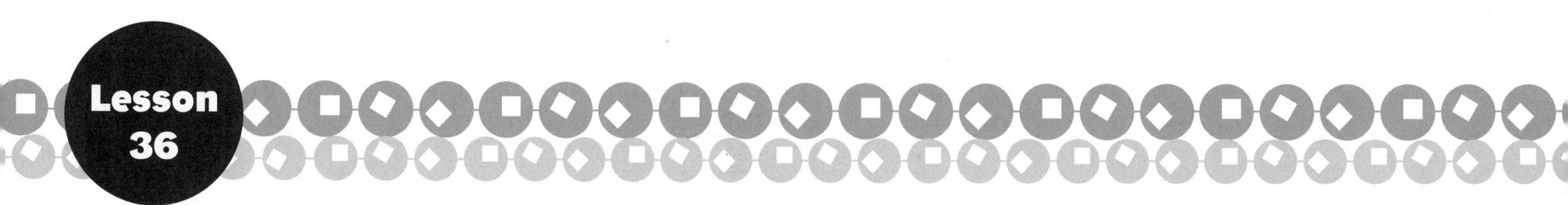

Blending Sounds into Words

red

this

sēē

big

ham

can

yet

man

fast

Blending Sounds into Words

this is ā big ham.
I can sēē thē ham.
it is red.

Lesson 36

Review: Letter-Sound Correspondences

r

h u a

sh

o

e

ē

s

ā th

Review: Blending Sounds into Words

ham

Letter-Sound Correspondences

y I v ō

a

e sh ē

m w

ā

th

h d s

Lesson 37

Blending Sounds into Words

gō

ship

shut

will

fast

wē

am

on

I

Lesson 37

Blending Sounds into Words

this is ā big ship.
it will gō fast.
wē can gō on thē ship.
I will gō on thē big ship.

Lesson 37

Review: Letter-Sound Correspondences

th r

y o sh

h

a

ē

p

w

s ā

y

Review: Blending Sounds into Words

shop

Letter-Sound Correspondences

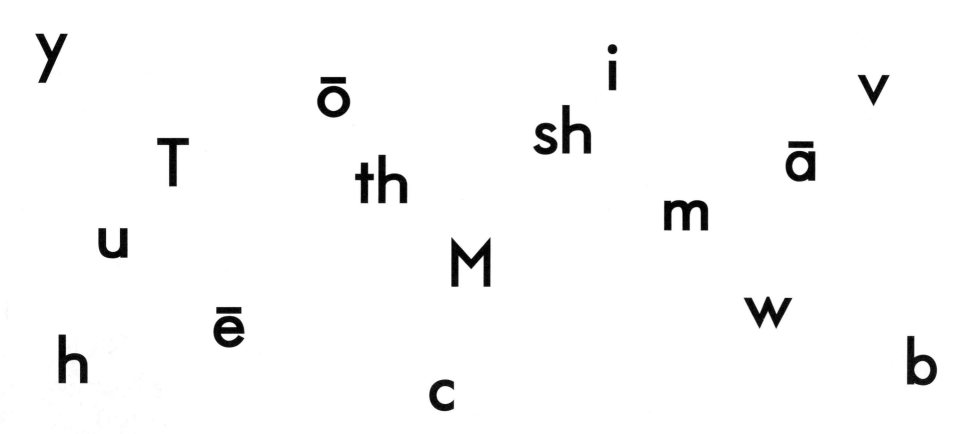

y ō i v

sh T ā th

m u M

w ē h b c

Lesson 38

Blending Sounds into Words

it

ship

grēēn

mē

on

gō

fast

sēē

Blending Sounds into Words

it is ā big grēēn ship.
thē ship will gō fast.
I am on thē ship.
sēē mē!

Lesson 38

Review: Letter-Sound Correspondences

c

o

b

w

e

ā

ē

th

sh

Review: Blending Sounds into Words

web

Lesson 39

Letter-Sound Correspondences

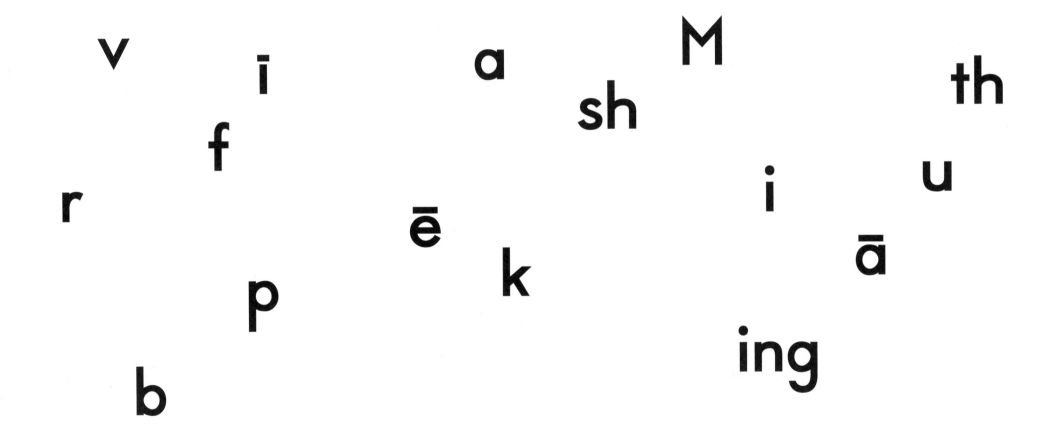

v ī a sh M th

f

r ē i u

k ā

p

ing

b

Lesson 39

Blending Sounds into Words

on

rīde

thē

līke

it

fun

sēē

Blending Sounds into Words

sēē mē rīde on thē ship.
it is fun <u>to</u> rīde on thē ship.
I līke it.

Lesson 39

Review: Letter-Sound Correspondences

e

sh

th

w

b

ā

c

ē

o

Review: Blending Sounds into Words

fun

Letter-Sound Correspondences

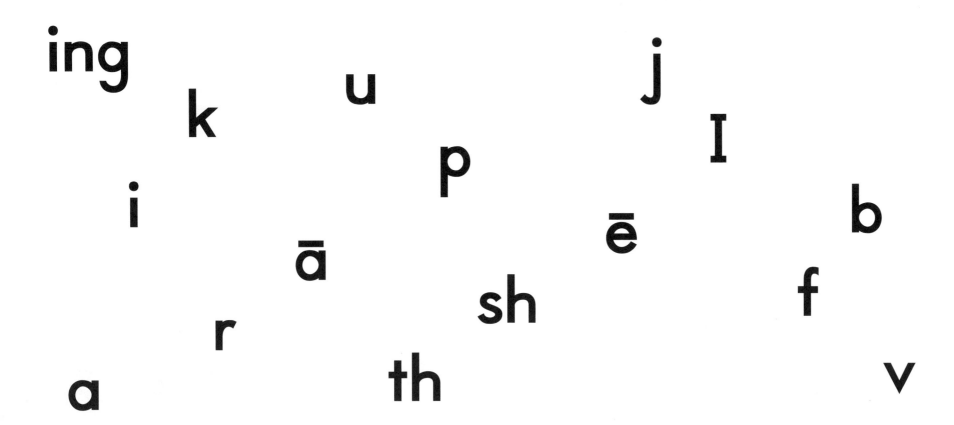

ing k u j I p i b ē ā sh f r a th v

Lesson 40

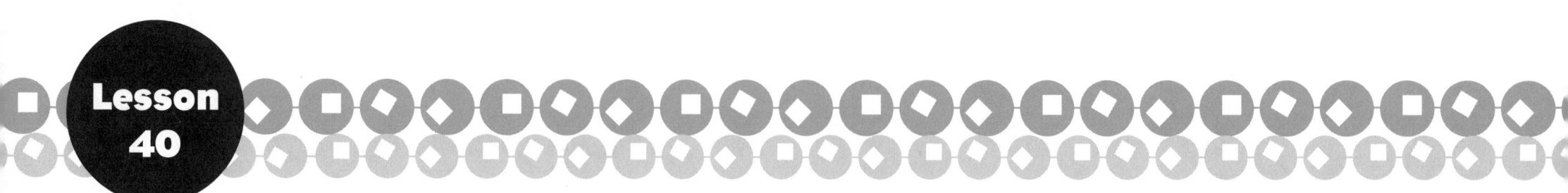

Blending Sounds into Words

run

frog

jump

thē

grēēn

grass

fast

will

gō

Blending Sounds into Words

thē grēēn frog will jump on thē grass.
it will jump fast.

Lesson 40

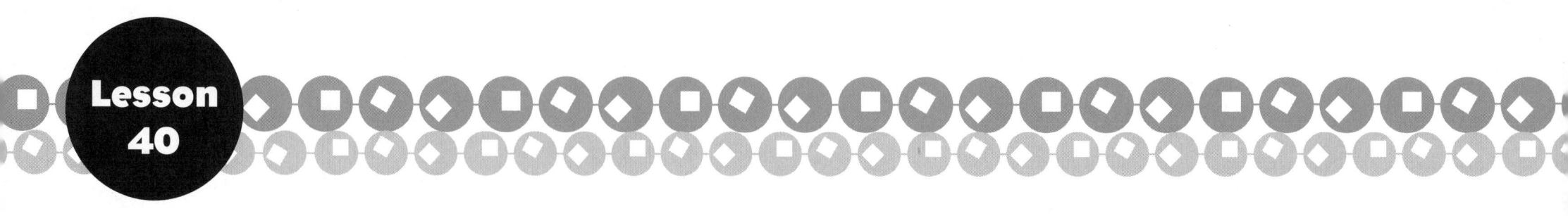

Blending Sounds into Words

thē frog cannot run.
gō, grēēn frog!
jump fast!

Mastery Test

Lessons 36–40

Letter-Sound Correspondences

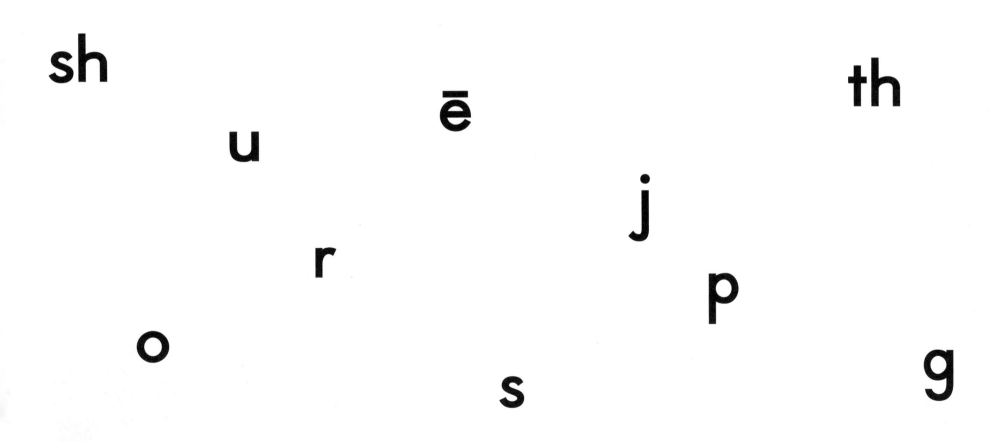

sh

u

ē

th

j

r

p

o

s

g

Lessons 36–40

Mastery Test

Blending Sounds into Words

run jump thē

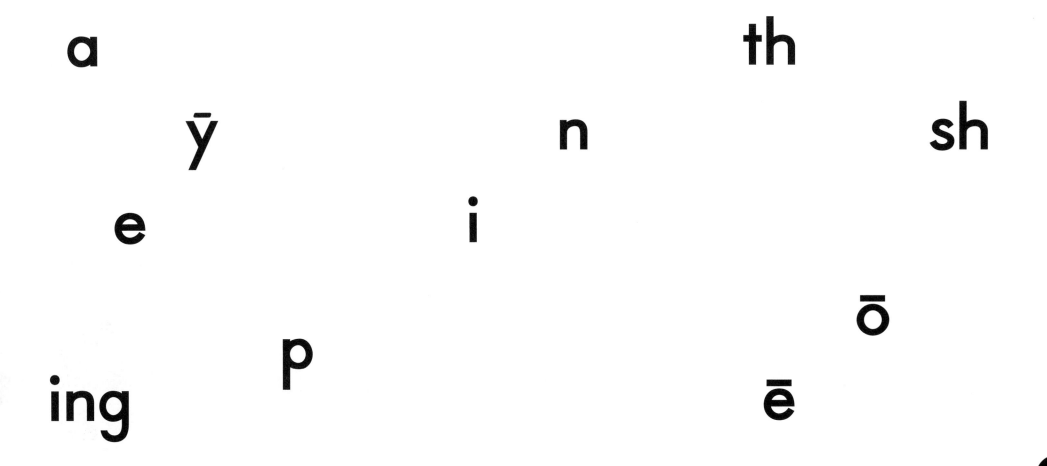

Letter-Sound Correspondences

a

th

ȳ

n

sh

e

i

ō

p

ing

ē

Lesson 41

Blending Sounds into Words

grēēn

mē

gō

run

can

jump

Review: Letter-Sound Correspondences

sh ing

i ā

e

r

th

ē

Review: Blending Sounds into Words

pot

Lesson 42

Letter-Sound Correspondences

g o

ȳ ing

c

n

ā

ī

j ō

Lesson 42

Blending Sounds into Words

līke

mȳ

nāme

jumping

gōing

Lesson 42

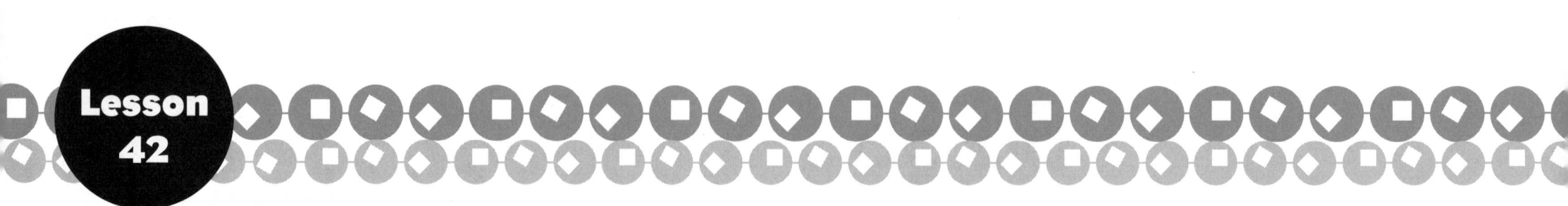

Review: Letter-Sound Correspondences

ō

a g

ī e

c i

ing

Review: Blending Sounds into Words

mȳ

Lesson 43

Letter-Sound Correspondences

s ā

o

k th

ing

r a

I ch ō

Lesson 43

Blending Sounds into Words

jumping

līke

ring

sing

run

thing

it

Lesson 43

Review: Letter-Sound Correspondences

ing

c e

g I

h ȳ

ī

Review: Blending Sounds into Words

rim

Lesson 44

Letter-Sound Correspondences

r

ch

ing

i

k

j

s

t

ō

Blending Sounds into Words

līke

singing

ramp

it

jumping

jump

sing

Lesson 44

Review: Letter-Sound Correspondences

ing ch

p

j

e

s t

ȳ

Review: Blending Sounds into Words

chop

Letter-Sound Correspondences

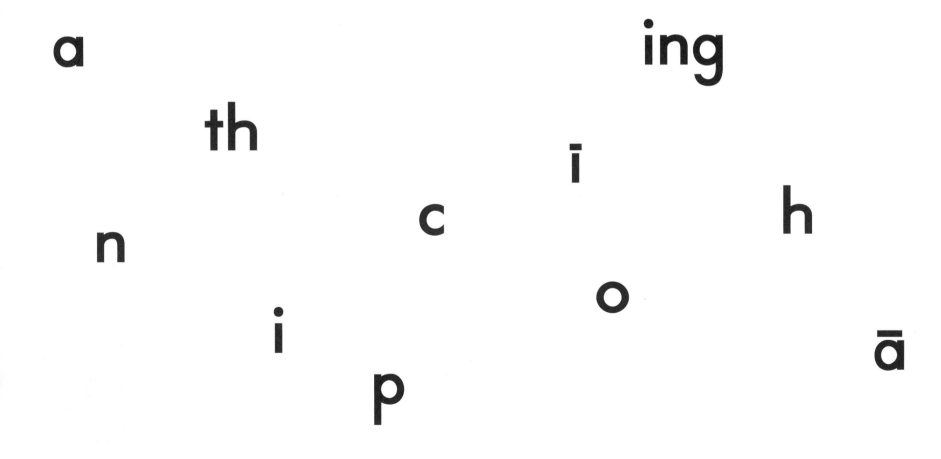

a

ing

th

ī

c

h

n

o

i

ā

p

Lesson 45

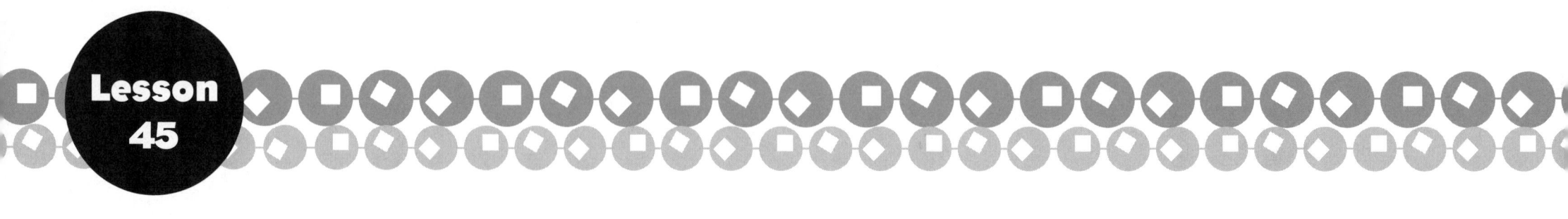

Blending Sounds into Words

sing

help

with

can

mē

singing

chop

helping

Mastery Test

Lessons 41–45

Letter-Sound Correspondences

e o

ō ā p

h

a

ing ē

Lessons 41–45

Mastery Test

Blending Sounds into Words

run   mē   can

Lesson 46

Letter-Sound Correspondences

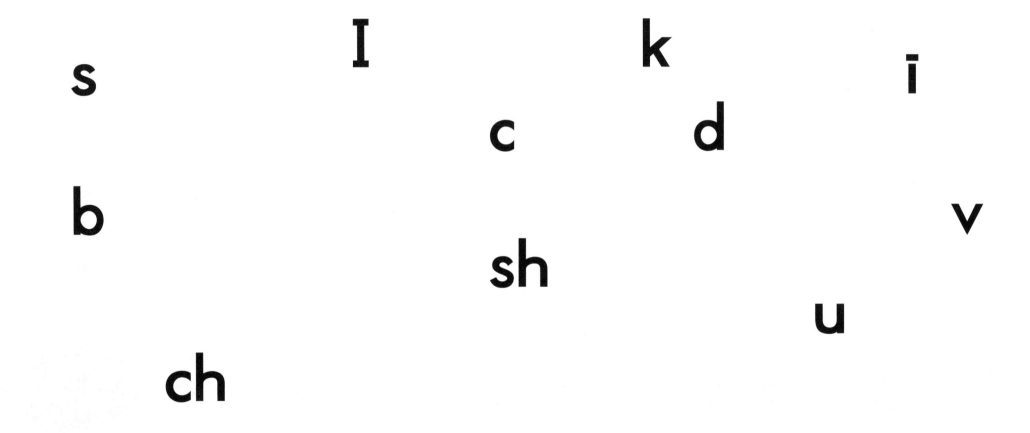

s

I

k

ī

c

d

b

v

sh

u

ch

Lesson 46

Blending Sounds into Words

fun

rīde

bīke

ship

bus

gō

ā

Lesson 46

Review: Letter-Sound Correspondences

k

v

e

d

u

ī

b

i

ē

t

Review: Blending Sounds into Words

bīke

ship

Lesson 46

Review: Sentence Reading

I can rīde ā bīke.

Letter-Sound Correspondences

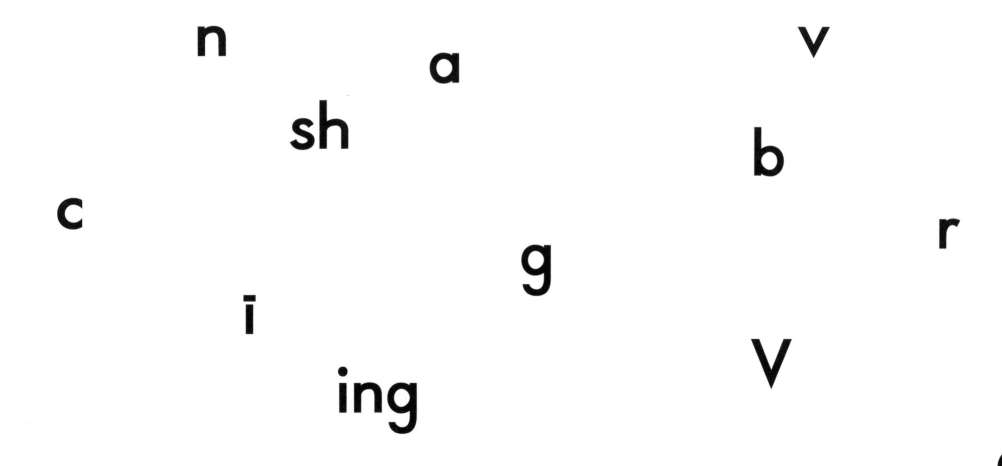

n

a

v

sh

b

c

r

g

i

V

ing

Lesson 47

Blending Sounds into Words

red

van

grēēn

on

ship

black

sēē

rīding

Review: Letter-Sound Correspondences

b v

sh

i c

j

ch

I t

Review: Blending Sounds into Words

bat

fast

Lesson 47

Review: Sentence Reading

thē black ship is fast.

Lesson 48

Letter-Sound Correspondences

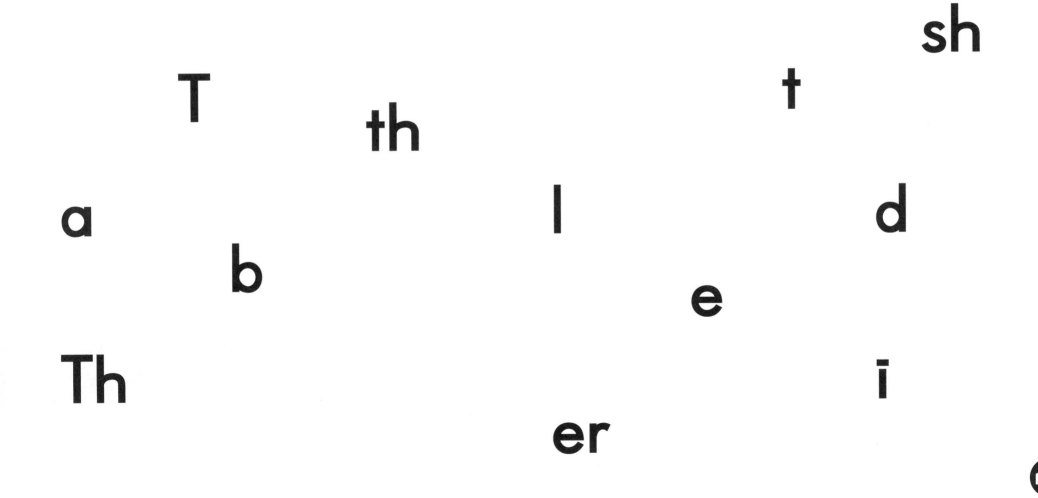

sh

T

t

th

a

l

d

b

e

Th

i

er

Lesson 48

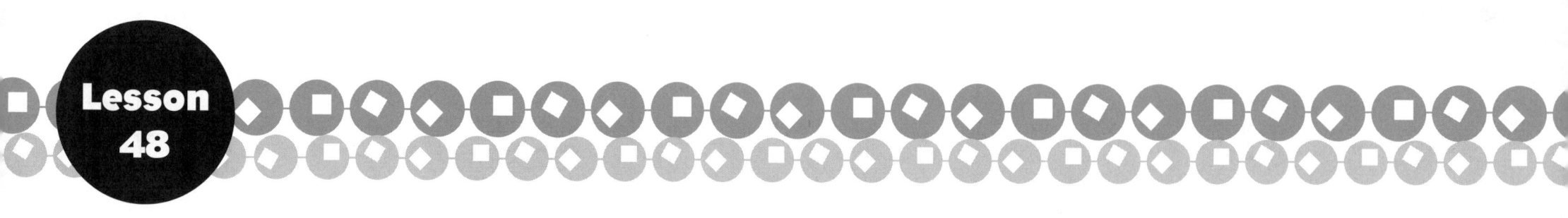

Blending Sounds into Words

and

stop

if

will

van

am

yet

gō

yes

bus

Lesson 48

Review: Letter-Sound Correspondences

sh

k

th

s

er

ō

Review: Blending Sounds into Words

yes

bus

stop

Lesson 48

Review: Sentence Reading

I will not stop.

Letter-Sound Correspondences

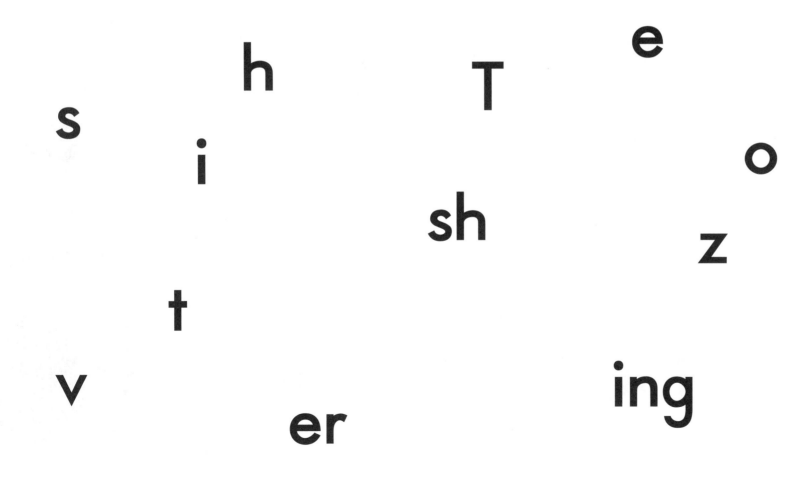

h T e

s

i o

sh

z

t

v ing

er

Lesson 49

Blending Sounds into Words

ship

on

hē

wāve

rīding

am

will

wāves

big

māke

Lesson 49

Review: Letter-Sound Correspondences

b

v

ī

T

s

h

z

Review: Blending Sounds into Words

māke

hē

wāve

Lesson 49

Review: Sentence Reading

hē will māke ā wāve.

Lesson 50

Letter-Sound Correspondences

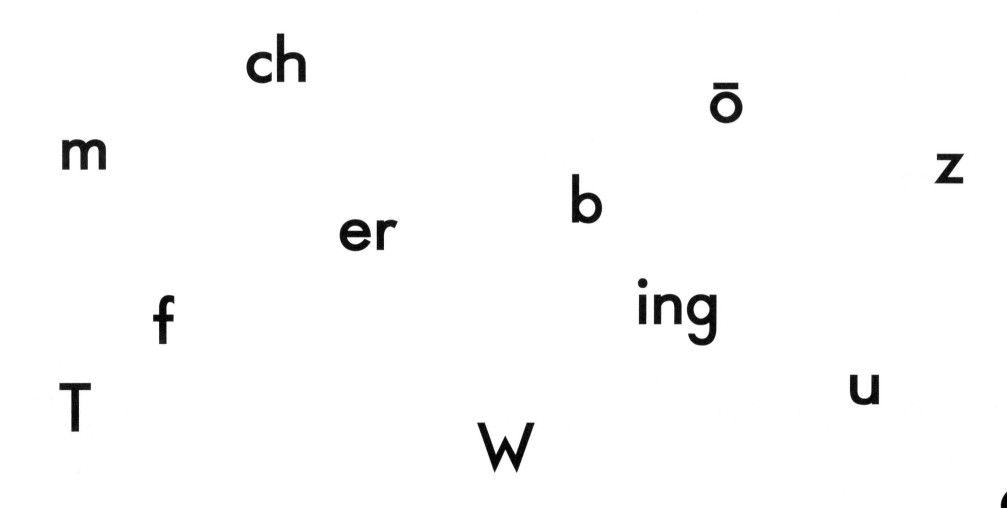

ch

ō

m

z

b

er

ing

f

u

T

W

Lesson 50

Blending Sounds into Words

fun

gō

wē

sit

fast

mȳ

much

bȳ

sō

sitting

Mastery Test

Lessons 46–50

Letter-Sound Correspondences

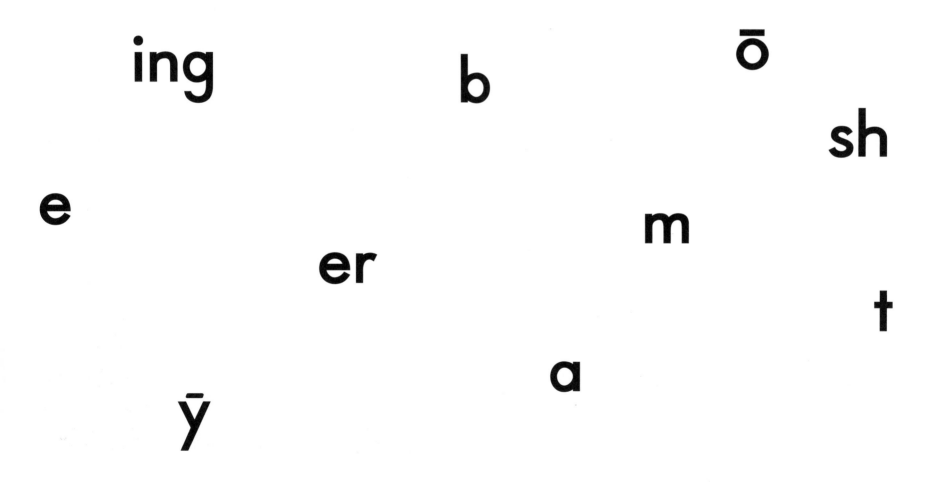

ing

b

ō

sh

e

m

er

t

a

ȳ

Lessons 46–50

Mastery Test

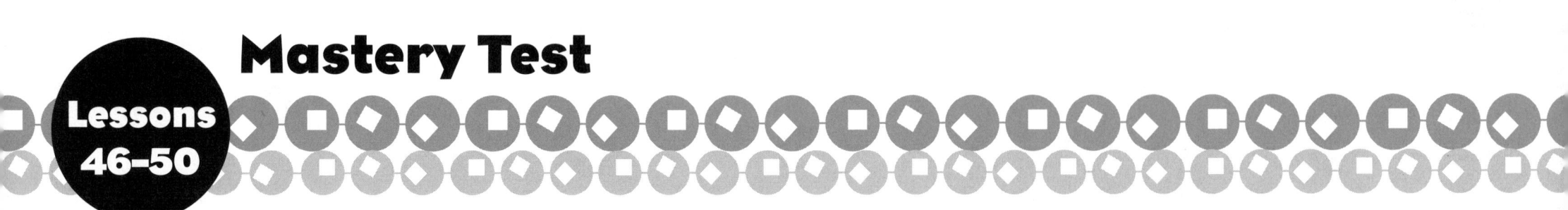

Blending Sounds into Words

bȳ   gō   mȳ

Sentence Reading

Sēē mē rīde on thē ship.

Letter-Sound Correspondences

x T t er

e

sh th p

m ch

P S

Lesson 51

Blending Sounds into Words

help

him

lunch

much

job

tāke

trash

Review: Letter-Sound Correspondences

er

ē

p

ch

m

sh

Review: Blending Sounds into Words

much

Review: Sentence Reading

I help fēēd thē dog.

Lesson 52

Letter-Sound Correspondences

x e ȳ

th er w c

m

W ē Y

Lesson 52

Blending Sounds into Words

and

with

fēēd

tāke

it

cāre

slēēp

him

Lesson 52

Review: Letter-Sound Correspondences

c ē

th

d

w

er z

Lesson 52

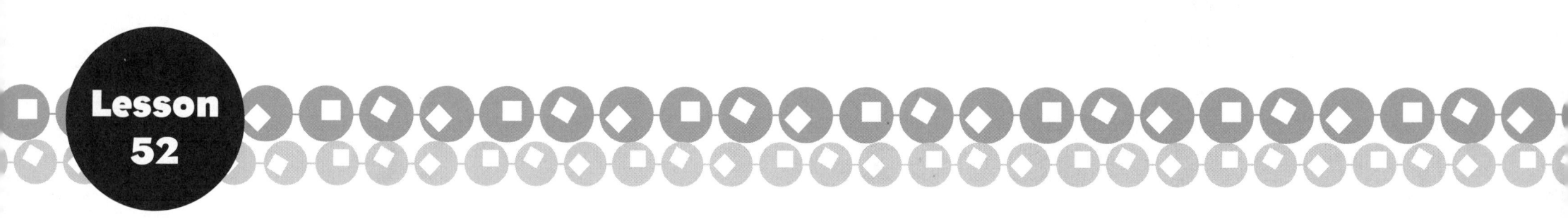

Review: Blending Sounds into Words

cāre   him   slēēp

Review: Sentence Reading

I help mȳ dog.

Lesson 53

Letter-Sound Correspondences

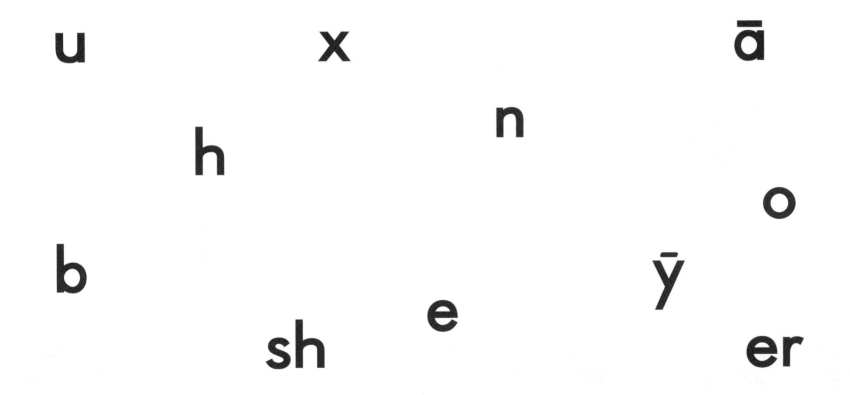

u x ā

h n

o

b ȳ

sh e er

Lesson 53

Blending Sounds into Words

stop

mȳ

egg

cāke

six

tāke

thē

bus

sister

Lesson 53

Review: Letter-Sound Correspondences

x

ā

o

ē

er

sh

Lesson 53

Review: Blending Sounds into Words

sister

help

Review: Sentence Reading

I help mȳ sister.

Lesson 54

Letter-Sound Correspondences

oo x

er I

h

sh b

s ȳ

t ā

Lesson 54

Blending Sounds into Words

box

sister

cāre

her

best

fix

stop

Lesson 54

Review: Letter-Sound Correspondences

u x ā

oo

h

b ȳ l

sh er

Lesson 54

Review: Blending Sounds into Words

box

sister

Review: Sentence Reading

Mȳ sister can fix the box.

Lesson 55

Letter-Sound Correspondences

t ā b

oo sh

I

ȳ er

x u

Lesson 55

Blending Sounds into Words

stop

fix

her

best

cāre

sister

box

Mastery Test

Lessons 51–55

Letter-Sound Correspondences

sh

ing

a

er

b

ō

m

ȳ

e

t

Mastery Test

Lessons 51-55

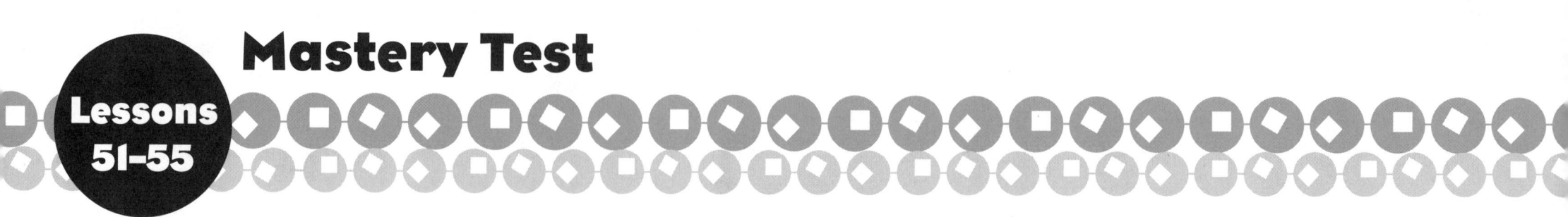

Blending Sounds into Words

her

Sentence Reading

I tāke cāre <u>of</u> ā dog.

Lesson 56

Letter-Sound Correspondences

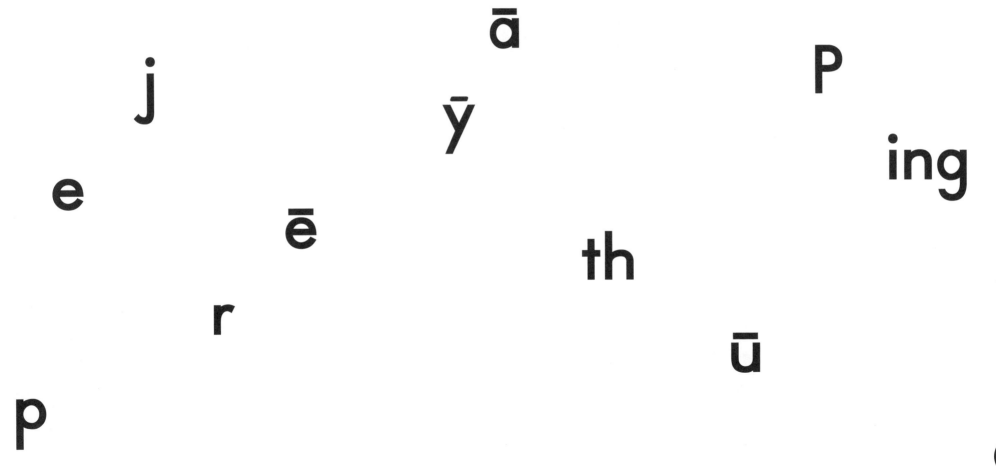

ā

j

P

ȳ

ing

e

ē

th

r

ū

p

Lesson 56

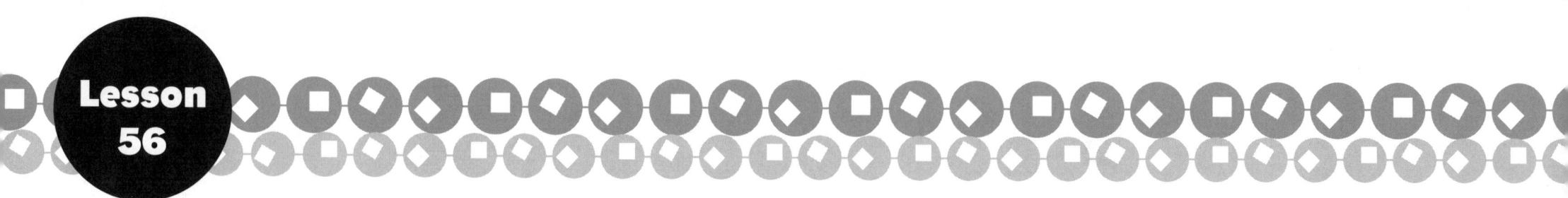

Blending Sounds into Words

pal's

is

rīding

running

sēē

nāme

bīke

jumping

Lesson 56

Review: Letter-Sound Correspondences

ū

p

ē

ī

r

l

Review: Blending Sounds into Words

run

thē

running

Lesson 56

Review: Sentence Reading

Mȳ pal can run and jump.

Lesson 57

Letter-Sound Correspondences

o

a

W

d

ū

c

s

w

e

I

Lesson 57

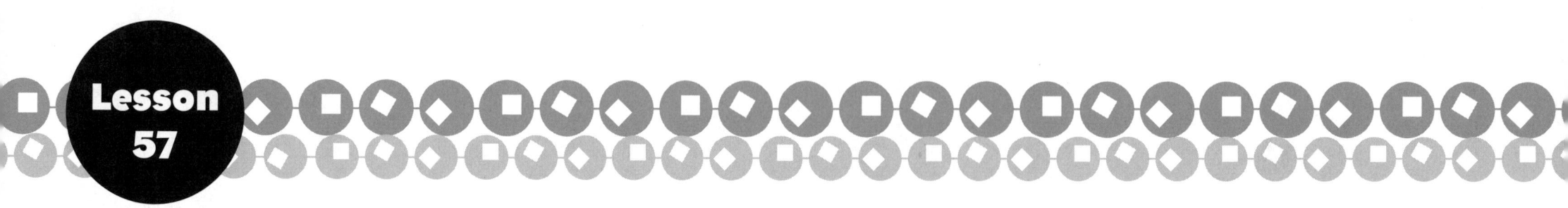

Blending Sounds into Words

can

and

lot

dog

swim

lāke

gets

dock

Lesson 57

Review: Letter-Sound Correspondences

i

u

ē

p

o

e

a

Lesson 57

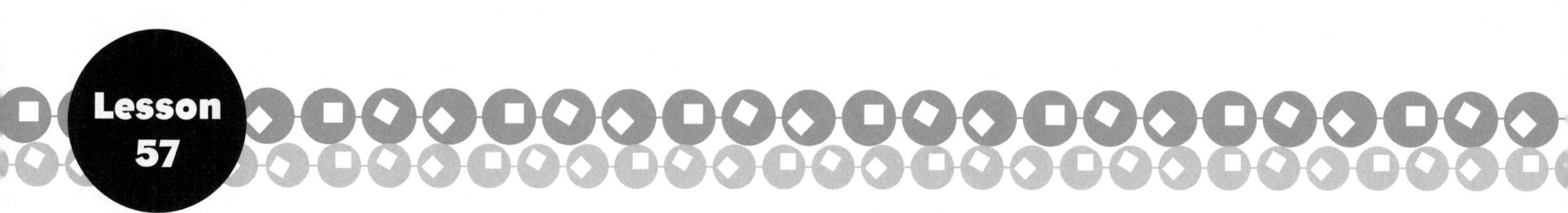

Review: Blending Sounds into Words

swim gets

Review: Sentence Reading

<u>You</u> can swim in thē big lāke.

Letter-Sound Correspondences

th

i b

M

l

T

ea

er

B

ū

sh

Lesson 58

Blending Sounds into Words

list

bē

rūles

ūsed

kīnd

bīte

bīt

rūle

Lesson 58

Review: Letter-Sound Correspondences

b

i

er

s

m

p

u

Lesson 58

Review: Blending Sounds into Words

fist   mash

Review: Sentence Reading

I can bē kīnd.

Lesson 59

Letter-Sound Correspondences

ch

d

sh

i

y

u

ēa

D

oo

Lesson 59

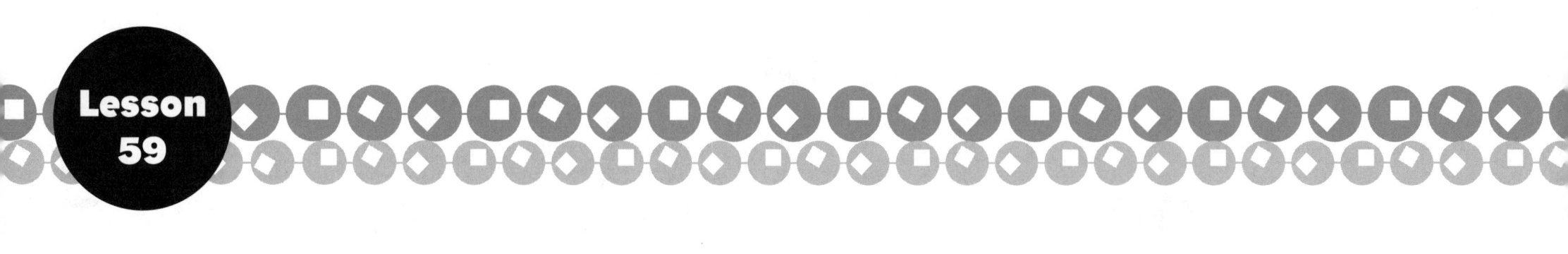

Blending Sounds into Words

chip

ēating

and

yum

yes

catch

ēat

chips

Lesson 59

Review: Letter-Sound Correspondences

ing

ch

x

er

sh

ēa

Lesson 59

Review: Blending Sounds into Words

sister   bunch

Review: Sentence Reading

I can ēat ā bunch <u>of</u> fish.

Lesson 60

Letter-Sound Correspondences

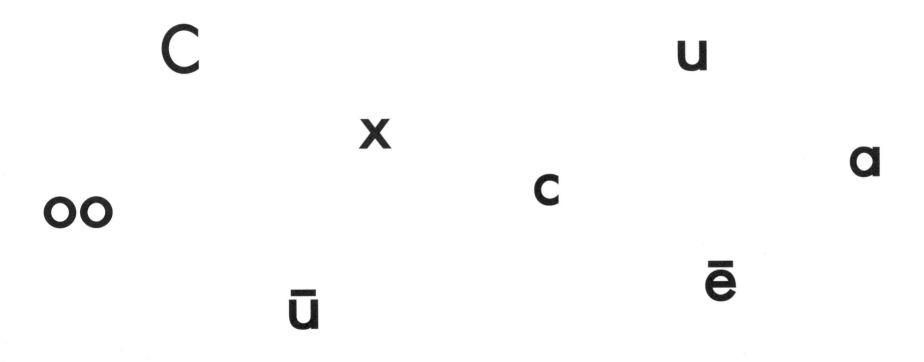

C

u

x

a

c

oo

ē

ū

Lesson 60

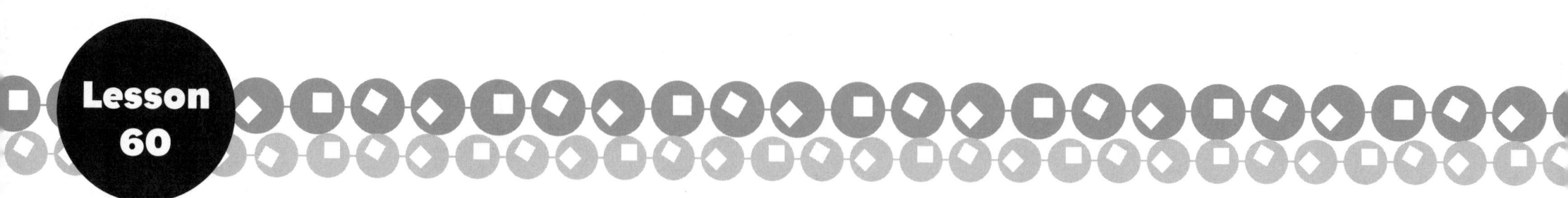

Blending Sounds into Words

soon

went

room

swim

with

cool

moon

swimming

Mastery Test

Lessons 56–60

Letter-Sound Correspondences

y C oo ū T sh th u x b

Lessons 56–60

Mastery Test

Blending Sounds into Words

swim　　went　　cool

Sentence Reading

Mȳ pal can rīde on ā big
grēēn fish.

Letter-Sound Correspondences

oo

ū

x

H

u

h

C

ea

Blending Sounds into Words

broom

clean

Lesson 61

Blending Sounds into Words: VCe Rules

game

hope

cube

here

smile

gate

Lesson 61

Review: Letter-Sound Correspondences

x oo u

ea

C ū

H ch

Lesson 61

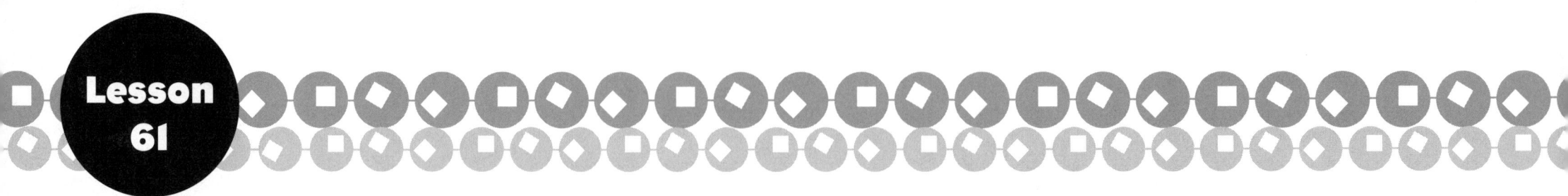

Review: Blending Sounds into Words

cheap yell jerk

Review: Sentence Reading

Thē bēē is flȳing in thē trēē.

Letter-Sound Correspondences

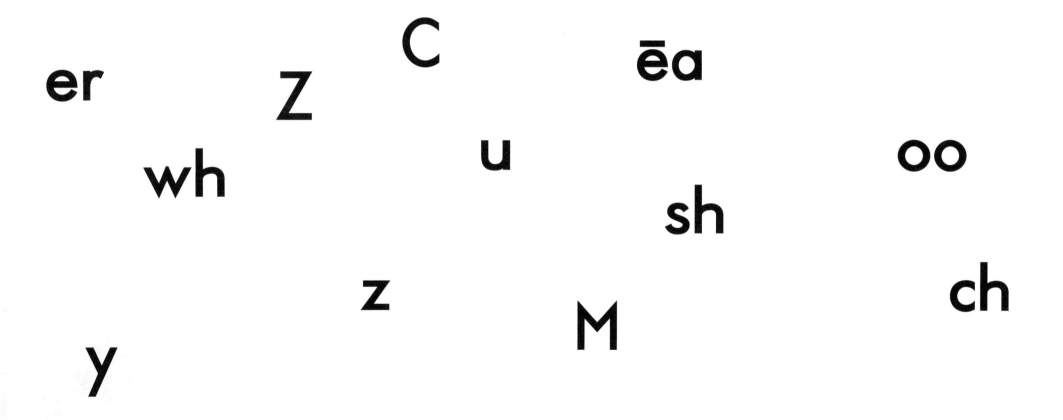

er Z C ēa u oo wh sh z ch M y

Lesson 62

Blending Sounds into Words

treat groom clean

Blending Sounds into Words: VCe Rules

wake rule

tote use life

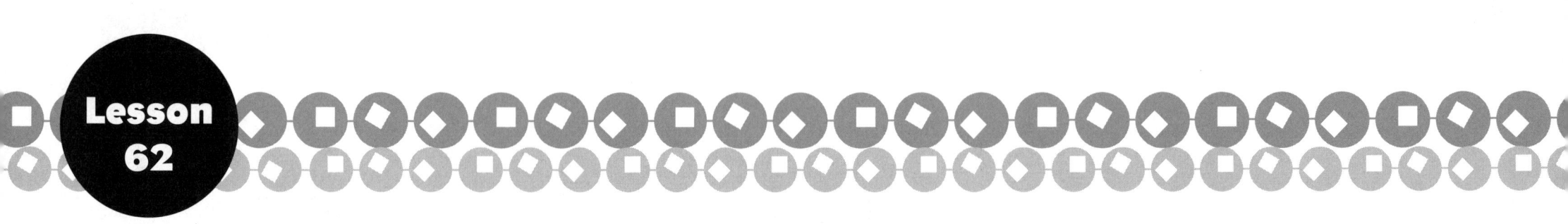

Lesson 62

Review: Letter-Sound Correspondences

oo

u

x

ēa

ū

Z

z

C

Lesson 62

Review: Blending Sounds into Words

meat boom

Review: Sentence Reading

I can eat lots <u>of</u> treats.

Lesson 63

Letter-Sound Correspondences

ou

D

wh

ū

x

Z

er

u

oo

Lesson 63

Blending Sounds into Words

whim

read

when

whiff

teacher

Blending Sounds into Words: VCe Rules

white

Dane

flute

Mike

smoke

Lesson 63

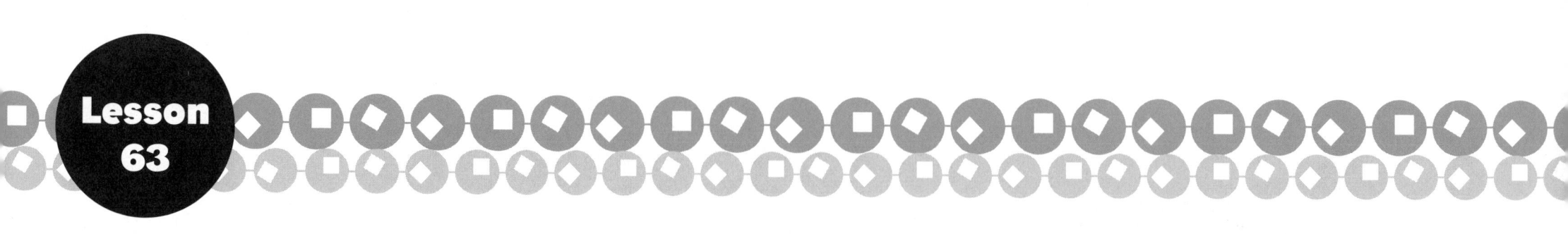

Review: Letter-Sound Correspondences

D u er wh x oo ū

Review: Blending Sounds into Words

heat Dan

Lesson 63

Review: Sentence Reading

The box is neat and clean.

Lesson 64

Letter-Sound Correspondences

M ar

ou

T h

b

ing

H

sh ch n

Lesson 64

Blending Sounds into Words

out

number

count

loud

Blending Sounds into Words: VCe Rules

hope

rake

hut

while

here

hop

Lesson 64

Review: Letter-Sound Correspondences

ar M ch sh

ing

h T

ou n wh

b

Review: Blending Sounds into Words

chart pout

Review: Sentence Reading

Mark and Barb found the park.

Lesson 65

Letter-Sound Correspondences

L ar B

ou T

b v y

wh w l

Blending Sounds into Words

sharp Lee

mouth dive

Lesson 65

Blending Sounds into Words: VCe Rules

tot

skate

cape

smile

cake

cap

tote

Lessons 61–65

Mastery Test

Letter-Sound Correspondences

wh

ar

ch

M

ou

sh

h

ing

b

n

T

Mastery Test

Lessons 61–65

Blending Sounds into Words

shouting March

Sentence Reading

Which chart did Tom and Barb make?

Lesson 66

Letter-Sound Correspondences

qu L ar ch

sh w h

wh

Blending Sounds into Words

Lee shine star

Carmen clouds

Lesson 66

Review: Letter-Sound Correspondences

L h sh

wh ch ar

w

Review: Blending Sounds into Words

whine booth

Lesson 66

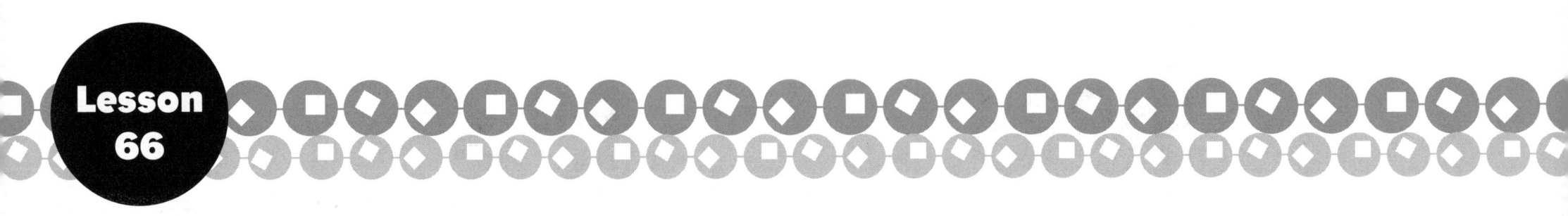

Review: Sentence Reading

The heat from the stove made the room warm.

Letter-Sound Correspondences

F ar f L

wh qu y v oo

Blending Sounds into Words

quit park

slide Barb swim

Lesson 67

Review: Letter-Sound Correspondences

ar L w

h sh

wh ch

Review: Blending Sounds into Words

quote stool

Lesson 67

Review: Sentence Reading

Pete had a kite with <u>three</u> red stripes and a white string.

Lesson 68

Letter-Sound Correspondences

oa ck qu

F

L

ar

wh

oo

ing

Lesson 68

Blending Sounds into Words

quill

darker

getting

swam

home

Lesson 68

Review: Letter-Sound Correspondences

F

L

oo

ing

ar

qu

wh

Review: Blending Sounds into Words

Fran

quite

Review: Sentence Reading

Mike made a card with white dots for his mom.

Lesson 69

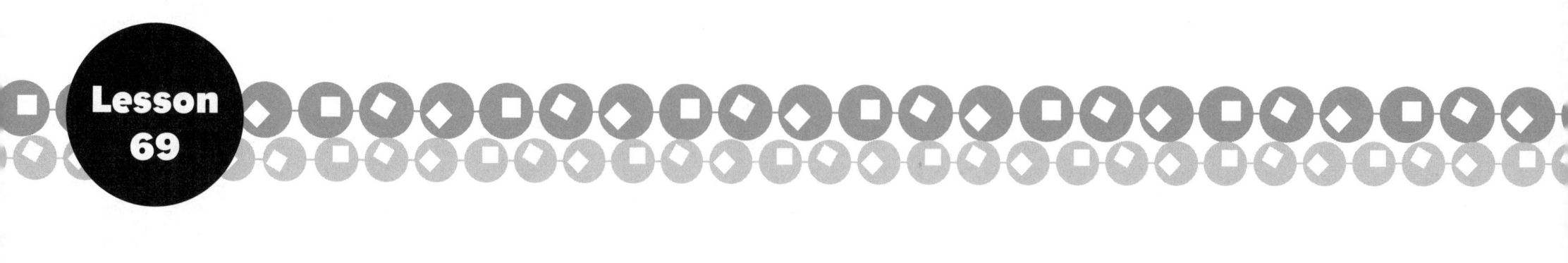

Letter-Sound Correspondences

z oa ck

qu sh

ing ar

Blending Sounds into Words

groan moon cheek

here bench

Lesson 69

Review: Letter-Sound Correspondences

oa

ck

qu

sh

ar

ing

Review: Blending Sounds into Words

boast

slick

Lesson 69

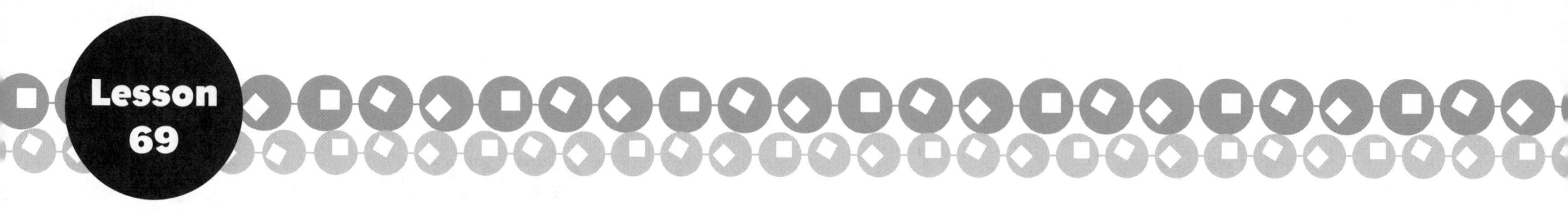

Review: Sentence Reading

The farmer left her coat in the barn when she went to feed the goat.

Letter-Sound Correspondences

z ee ck wh

ch oa qu

Blending Sounds into Words

zipper quack

Zig

smiles reach

Lessons 66-70

Mastery Test

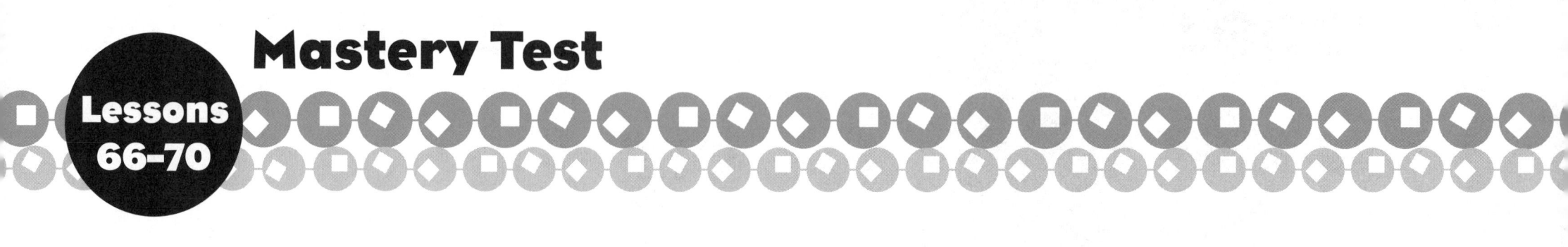

Letter-Sound Correspondences

ch qu wh

z

ck oa

Blending Sounds into Words

Zack coach

Mastery Test

Lessons 66–70

Sentence Reading

The lime had a lot of zest
when he ate it.

Lesson 71

Letter-Sound Correspondences

H

z

ee

oa

qu

wh

n

ch

ar

N

Blending Sounds into Words

Fred

Buzz

bee

teach

toad

read

Lesson 71

Review: Letter-Sound Correspondences

ee z N

wh

oa

qu

ing

ch

F ar L

Review: Blending Sounds into Words

Flop

quote

sheet

While

Coast

Review: Sentence Reading

The smart shark quit eating
slime with his sharp teeth.

Lesson 72

Letter-Sound Correspondences

H ai ee oa

z qu ar oo

Blending Sounds into Words

bee

toad

Fred

Buzz

Review: Letter-Sound Correspondences

H

wh

oo

ar

qu

z

ee

oa

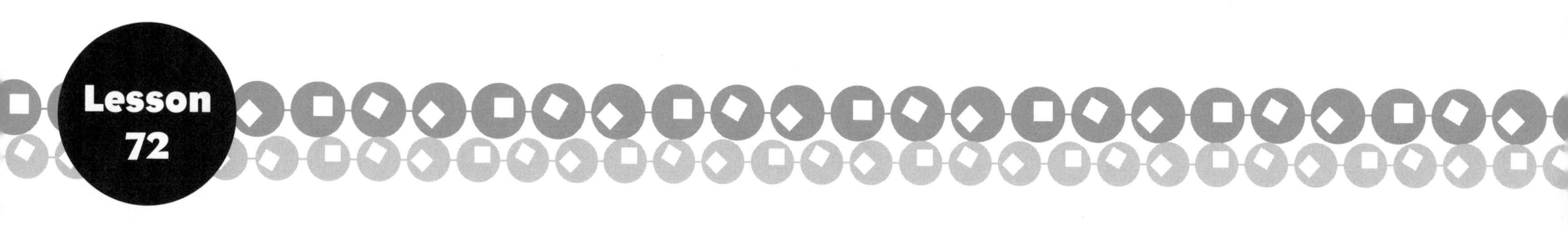

Lesson 72

Review: Blending Sounds into Words

sweet smooch boat

whiff tar

Review: Sentence Reading

The goat had green teeth in his mouth from eating too much grass.

Lesson 73

Letter-Sound Correspondences

G g oo qu

ai z oa ee F

Blending Sounds into Words

reading finger air

out check sound

Lesson 73

Review: Letter-Sound Correspondences

f ai oo qu

oa ee z

Review: Blending Sounds into Words

paint feet

Review: Sentence Reading

Zack made a boat to float in the great green pool.

Lesson 74

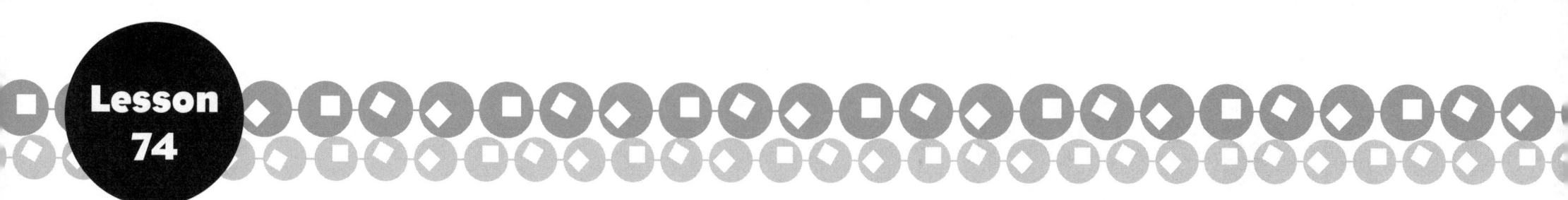

Letter-Sound Correspondences

or ai oo G oa z ee wh

Blending Sounds into Words

smart air sounds chart

Lesson 74

Review: Letter-Sound Correspondences

G ee ai oa

oo wh

Review: Blending Sounds into Words

float street

air sounds

chair chart

Lesson 74

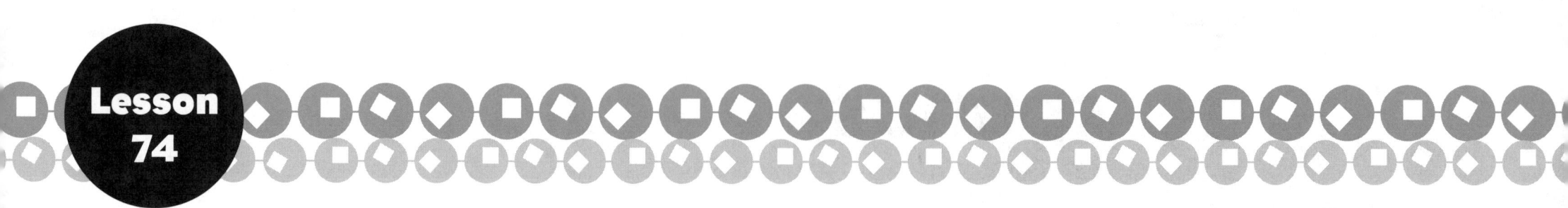

Review: Sentence Reading

Greg can chain the goat to the tree in the yard and feed it, too.

Lesson 75

Letter-Sound Correspondences

z

or

ai

oa

ee

oo

G

Blending Sounds into Words

neat

hive

queen

king

jobs

Lessons 71-75

Mastery Test

Letter-Sound Correspondences

or Z ai oo

ee oa

Blending Sounds into Words

porch snail

boot

sleep loan

Mastery Test

Sentence Reading

The zipper was torn off her coat, so she felt the cool air on her neck.

Lesson 76

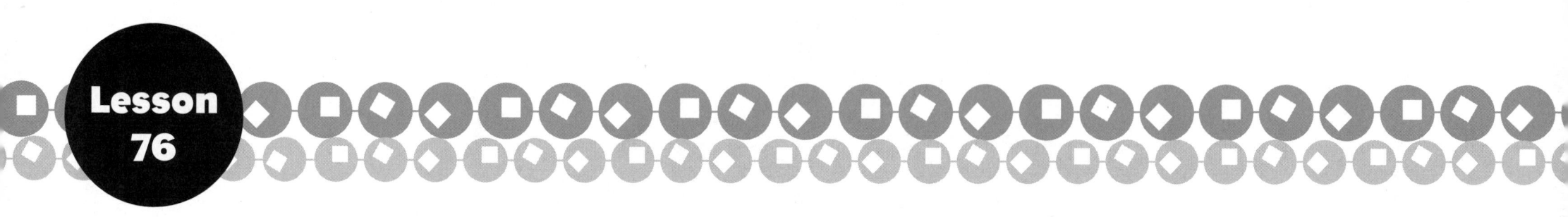

Letter-Sound Correspondences

ol ai oa ee z

G oo or ar

Blending Sounds into Words

trail mail hard

north wheels

track

Lesson 76

Review: Letter-Sound Correspondences

ai oa ee z

or oo ar

Review: Blending Sounds into Words

wheel moon float

stair quiz Mars

Lesson 76

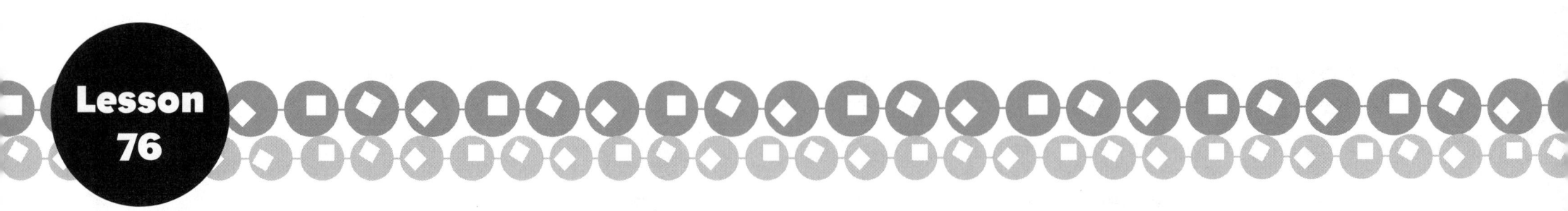

Review: Sentence Reading

He tore his shorts on the rail of the porch as he went up the stairs.

Letter-Sound Correspondences

R or ol

ai oa

ee z ar

oo

Lesson 77

Blending Sounds into Words

mail

going

getting

fear

forming

Review: Letter-Sound Correspondences

ar　or　oo　ee

oa　ai　ol

Review: Blending Sounds into Words

bold　tail　load

weed　boot　arm

fort

Lesson 77

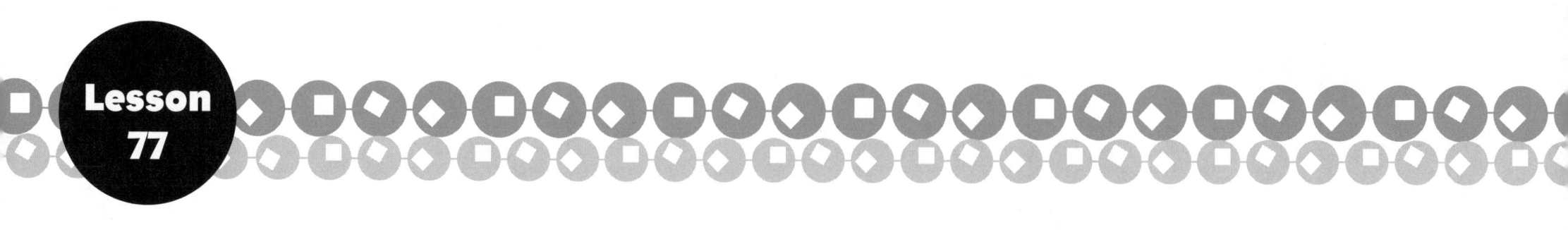

Review: Sentence Reading

The seal was born on the shore of the sea.

Lesson 78

Letter-Sound Correspondences

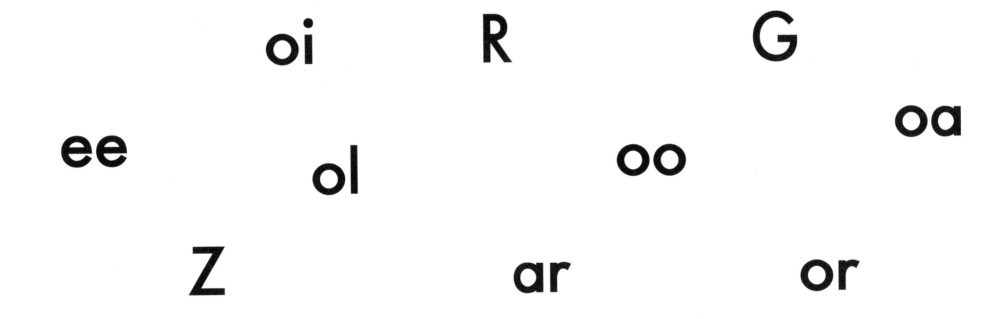

oi R G

ee ol oo oa

Z ar or

Lesson 78

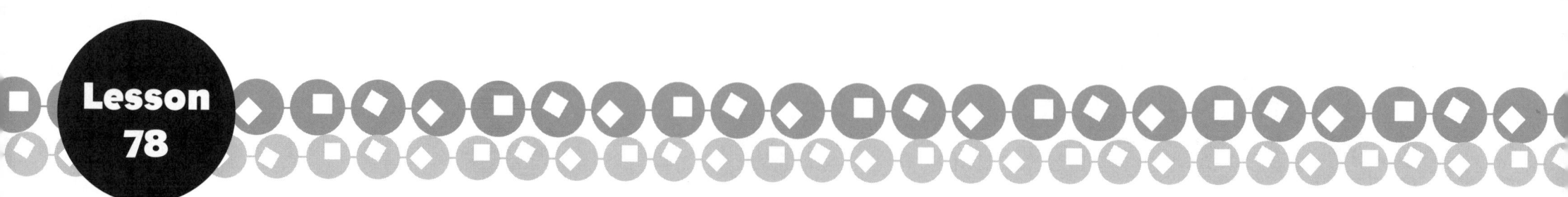

Blending Sounds into Words

rails

feel

track

rain

snort

steam

sound

Lesson 78

Review: Letter-Sound Correspondences

R ar ol or

oo ee oa ai

Review: Blending Sounds into Words

Russ gold main

toast tree

cool Mort Carl

Lesson 78

Review: Sentence Reading

Russ made his coach a neat pair of shorts in class.

Lesson 79

Letter-Sound Correspondences

E ee oi

R ol

ar oa

oo or

Z

Lesson 79

Blending Sounds into Words

colt

weak

slick

steep

track

Lesson 79

Review: Letter-Sound Correspondences

oi R ol ai

oa oo or

Review: Blending Sounds into Words

roast flair old

float shoot torch

Lesson 79

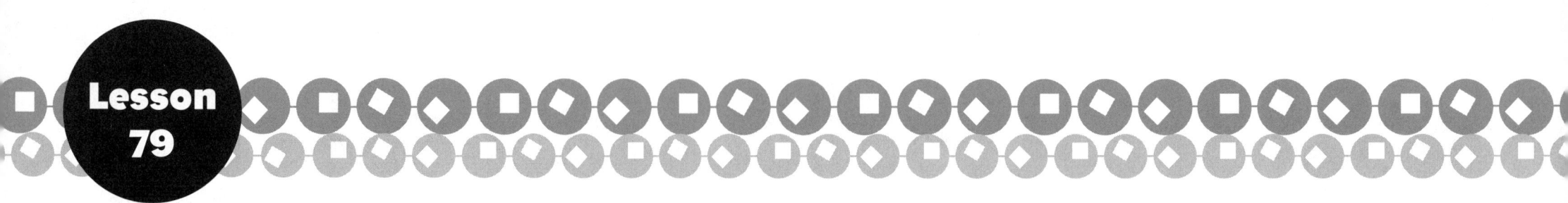

Review: Sentence Reading

It is too cold to use the roller to paint the roof gold.

Letter-Sound Correspondences

oy E Z

R oi ol

ai

oo

or ea

Lesson 80

Blending Sounds into Words

steam

Faith

bold

crept

slick

wheels

Mastery Test

Lessons 76–80

Letter-Sound Correspondences

E oi R ol

ai oo ck

Blending Sounds into Words

Ed coin Red

short pain

pool flick

Lessons 76-80

Mastery Test

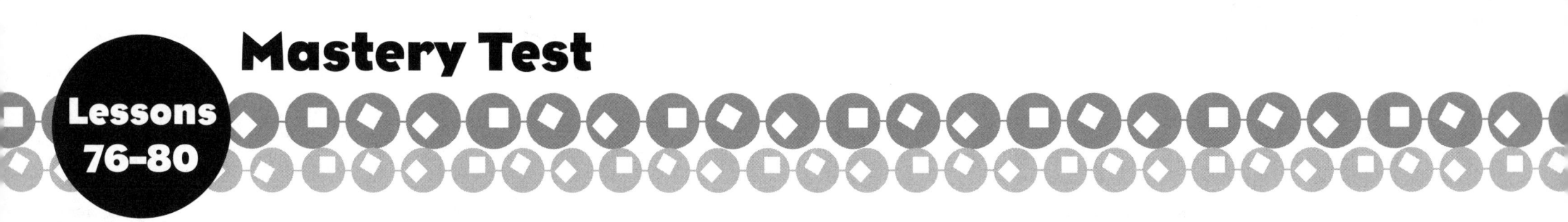

Sentence Reading

Her little friend has some paint, beads, and beans for the craft in the art room.

Lesson 81

Letter-Sound Correspondences

a oy E oi

ar

R ai oo

Blending Sounds into Words

Troy coin

gold Floyd

Lesson 81

Review: Letter-Sound Correspondences

wh ar oo

ai R

E oi oy

Review: Blending Sounds into Words

oil Ed joy

whiff jar Roy broom

Review: Sentence Reading

The boy felt the cool rain in the crisp March air.

Lesson 82

Letter-Sound Correspondences

ir ur er

a oy

oi E oo

Blending Sounds into Words

team join Troy

gold coin Lee

Lesson 82

Review: Letter-Sound Correspondences

ee oa oo

oi oy

Review: Blending Sounds into Words

Roy joint bloom

loaf feed

Lesson 82

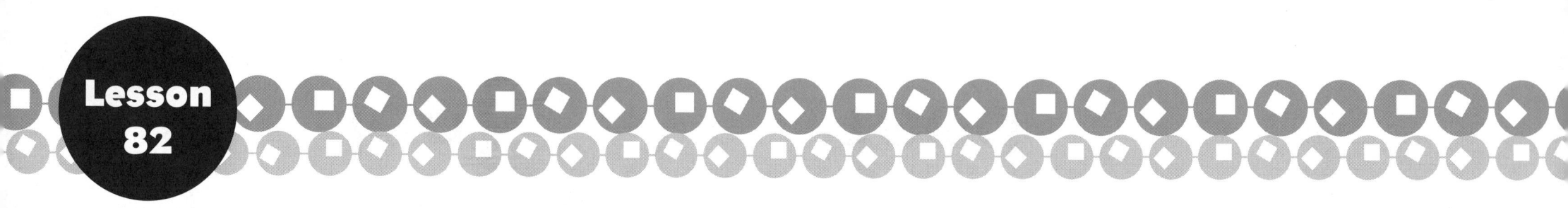

Review: Sentence Reading

The goat ate the weeds in the front yard for three weeks.

Lesson 83

Letter-Sound Correspondences

ow ir oy E

oo ur a

Blending Sounds into Words

ground

dirt squirt

Lesson 83

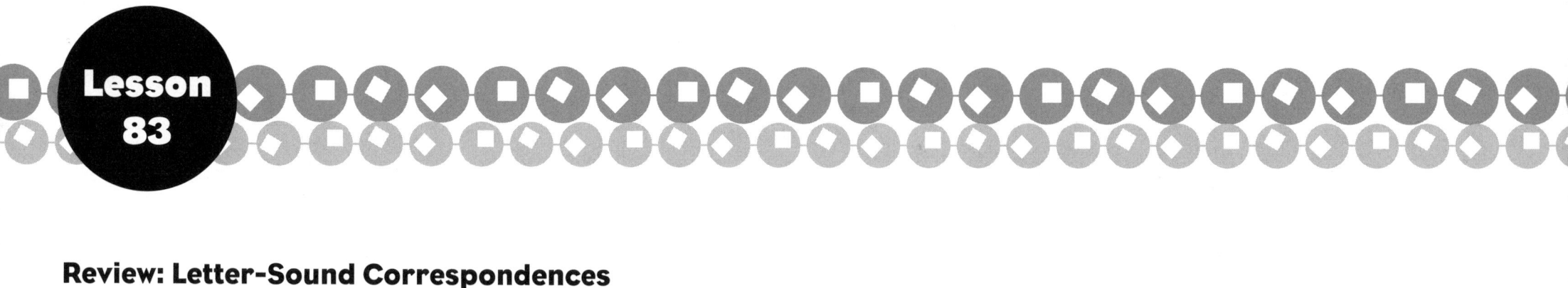

Review: Letter-Sound Correspondences

ir er ur

a oy oo

Review: Blending Sounds into Words

clearer smirk moon

turn ad toys

Review: Sentence Reading

Ed had a fork and a spoon to eat the plate of sweet food.

Lesson 84

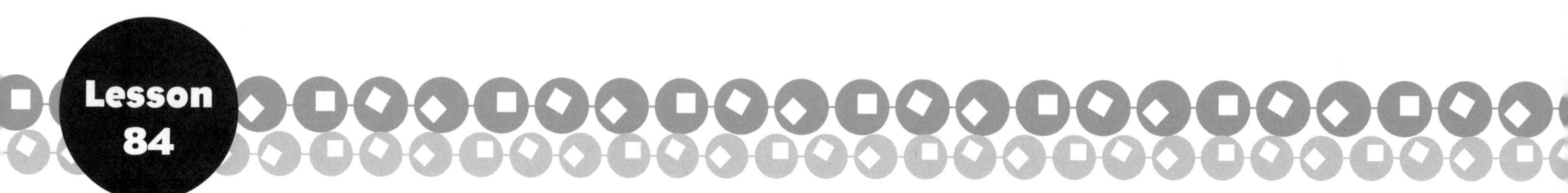

Letter-Sound Correspondences

N ow z

oy ol or

ir E ur a

Blending Sounds into Words

share matter

stirring hurt

Lesson 84

Review: Letter-Sound Correspondences

ir ur

er oy

ol oo

Review: Blending Sounds into Words

slow roller bold

burnt whirl hoist

Lesson 84

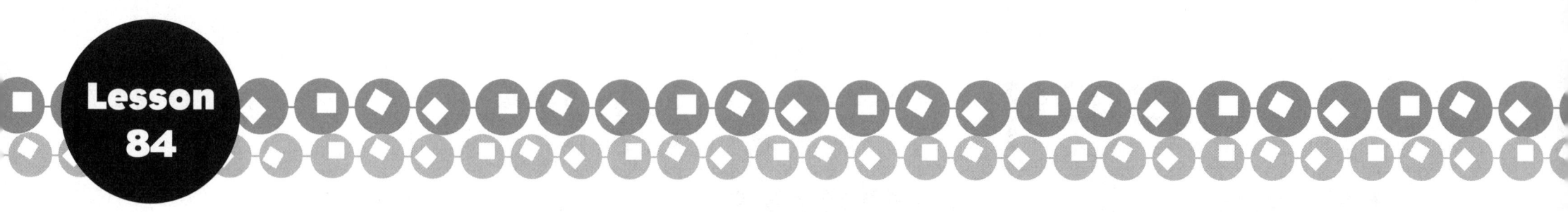

Review: Sentence Reading

Throw me the scarf and the coat for the freezing rain and snow.

Letter-Sound Correspondences

igh N ur a

ow ir z

Blending Sounds into Words

neat hive

queen

king jobs

Mastery Test

Lessons 81-85

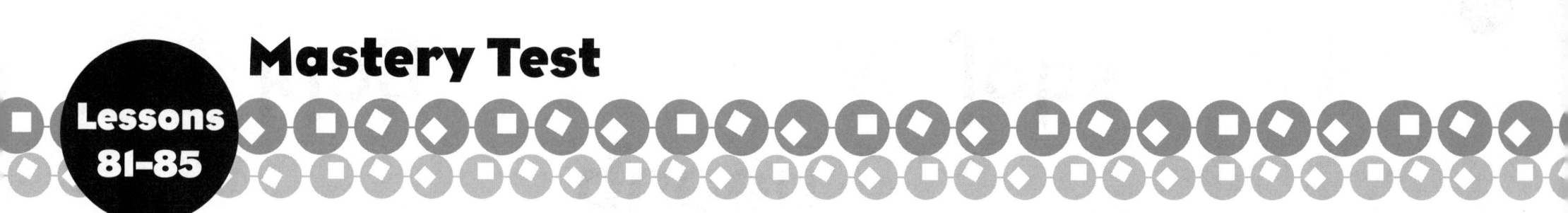

Letter-Sound Correspondences

ow a

z ir ur

Blending Sounds into Words

grown smirk

lurch

Ann zipper

Mastery Test

Lessons 81-85

Sentence Reading

The trooper saw the boys speeding through Choy Street.

Lesson 86

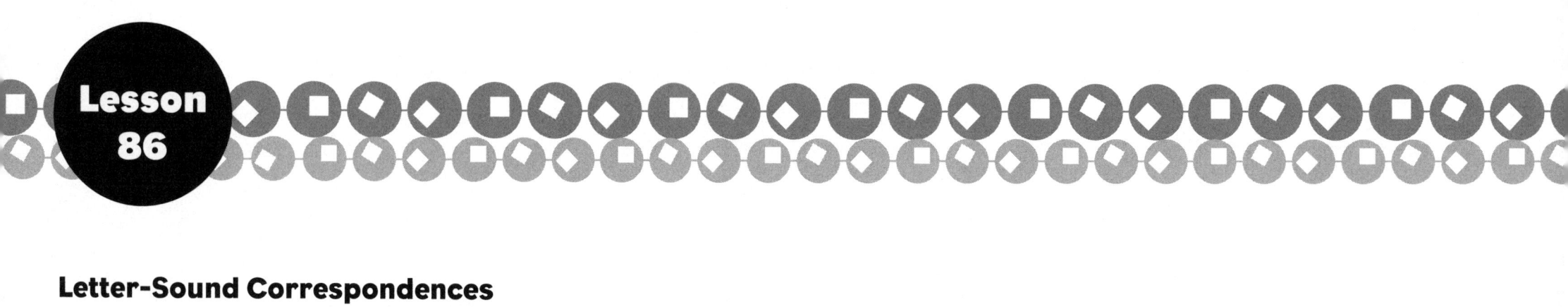

Letter-Sound Correspondences

ay igh N ow

ir ur oy

R oi

Blending Sounds into Words

fire boots fighter

burning girls

Lesson 86

Review: Letter-Sound Correspondences

igh N ow ir

ur oy R oi

Review: Blending Sounds into Words

sight Ned crow

Rust Kirk

burst joys oil

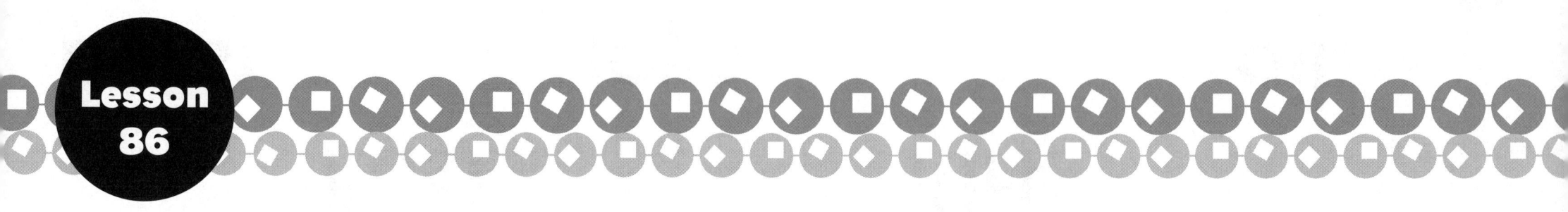

Review: Sentence Reading

Ned saw his mother stirring cake mix as he turned the corner.

Lesson 87

Letter-Sound Correspondences

J ay igh

N ow oy

Blending Sounds into Words

Turner barn

Street goat

weeping burning

Lesson 87

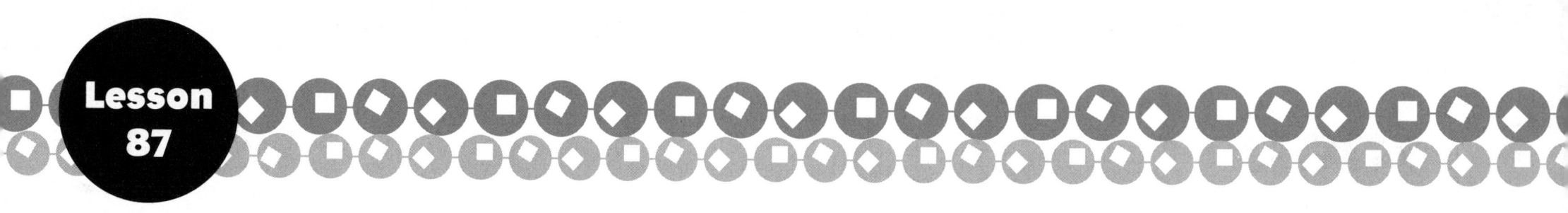

Review: Letter-Sound Correspondences

ay ow N igh

ir ur

Review: Blending Sounds into Words

stay right

Ness

show smirk churn

Review: Sentence Reading

May I go to the show to see the girls and boys who swing high in the air and the seal that does flips?

Lesson 88

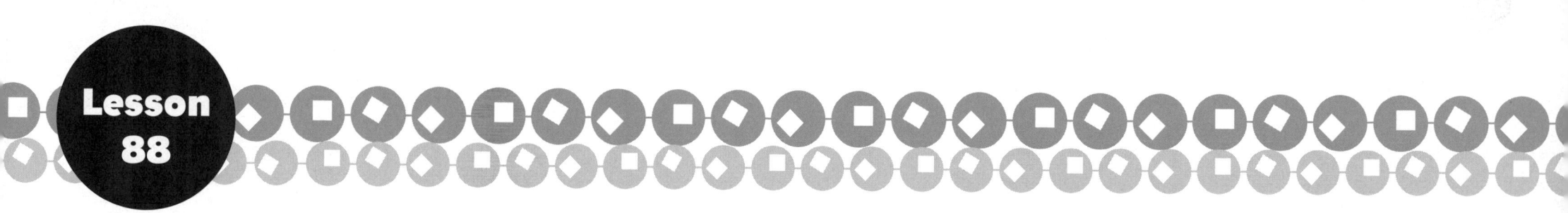

Letter-Sound Correspondences

au   aw   J

ay   igh   N   ol

Blending Sounds into Words

ropes   tight

cannot

spray   necks

Lesson 88

Review: Letter-Sound Correspondences

oo oa

ea ee igh

Review: Blending Sounds into Words

mood roach

stream

streets might

Lesson 88

Review: Sentence Reading

Did you speak to Jean about the show next week?

Lesson 89

Letter-Sound Correspondences

ew igh J

au aw ay

Blending Sounds into Words

spraying rooster

rafters

ladder reach flames

Lesson 89

Review: Letter-Sound Correspondences

or ai

oo oa

ay aw au

Review: Blending Sounds into Words

order flair

stoop moan

crayon stray

flaw vault

Review: Sentence Reading

I want to inform you that it is not my fault that I broke the seesaw.

Lesson 90

Letter-Sound Correspondences

ph ew ir a au

a aw J ay igh

Blending Sounds into Words

lawn smolder

kindness

spraying

Lessons 86-90

Mastery Test

Letter-Sound Correspondences

aw

oi

au

oo

ee

or

ar

J

Mastery Test

Blending Sounds into Words

August

straw

foil

jeep

border

farther

Jeff

Lessons 86-90

Mastery Test

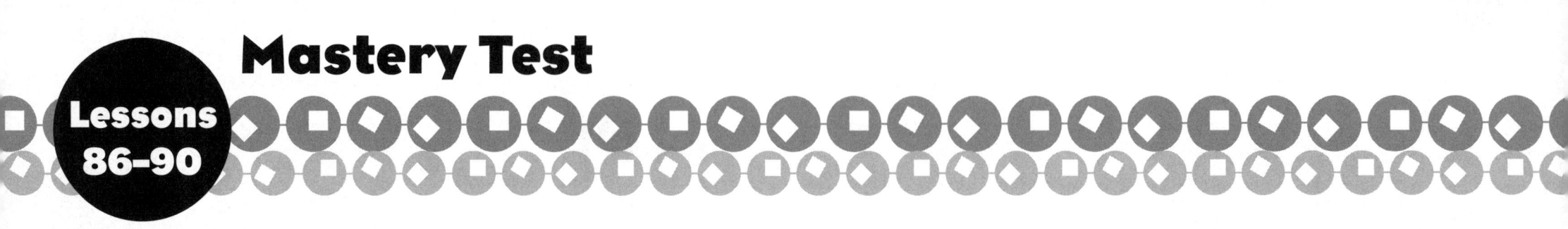

Sentence Reading

The panda was chewing a stick of beautiful green bamboo in the forest.

Lesson 91

Letter-Sound Correspondences

kn ph ew au

aw J ow

Blending Sounds into Words

Phil pillow June tide

flowing dunes

Andrew

Lesson 91

Review: Letter-Sound Correspondences

a ur ir

igh

ay J

aw au

ph ew

Lesson 91

Review: Blending Sounds into Words

shirt

cheese

phone

flew

fault

Jed

straw

play

might

Ashton

Lesson 91

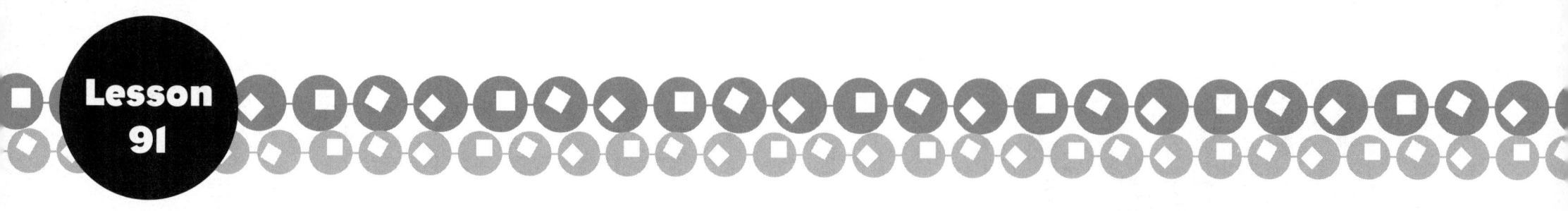

Review: Sentence Reading

Ralph saw a crawfish digging in the dirt by the side of the river.

Lesson 92

Letter-Sound Correspondences

wr kn ph

ew au

aw ay

N igh

Lesson 92

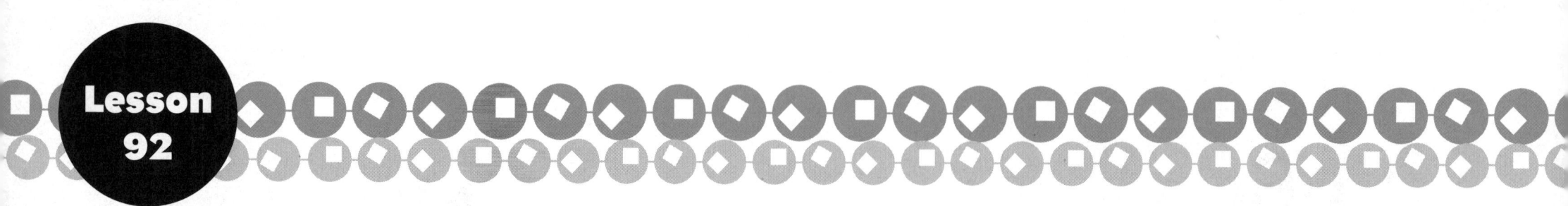

Blending Sounds into Words

forth

dolphins

whales

blowing

spouts

fellow

Lesson 92

Review: Letter-Sound Correspondences

ay aw au

ew ph kn

Review: Blending Sounds into Words

knot sphere Lew

fraud shawl May

Lesson 92

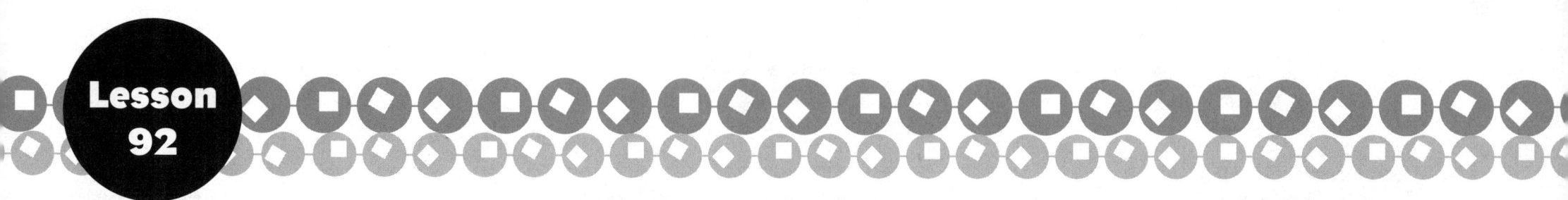

Review: Sentence Reading

My teacher's name is Paul Phillips, and he is from Austin, Texas.

Lesson 93

Letter-Sound Correspondences

igh ay aw ew

ph

kn wr

Letter-Sound Correspondences

ed

Lesson 93

Blending Sounds into Words

minnows

lobsters

seagulls

postcards

Lesson 93

Review: Letter-Sound Correspondences

ay wr aw

kn ph ew

Review: Blending Sounds into Words

wrap know

phone flew

flaw tray

Lesson 93

Review: Sentence Reading

A hawk flew higher and higher in the air until it was out of sight.

Lesson 94

Letter-Sound Correspondences

igh ay aw au

ew ph

wr kn

Letter-Sound Correspondences

ed

Lesson 94

Blending Sounds into Words

phew

sunburn

cooling

cream

Lesson 94

Review: Letter-Sound Correspondences

ph

wr

kn

aw

au

ew

Lesson 94

Review: Blending Sounds into Words

Paul

crawl

blew

graph

wrist

know

Review: Sentence Reading

Paul Phillips got a new crew cut when he went to join the swim team.

Lesson 95

Letter-Sound Correspondences

ace kn

wr

ph ew au

ay igh

Letter-Sound Correspondences

ed

Lesson 95

Letter-Sound Correspondences

kissed

jumped

nested

smelled

packed

granted

Lesson 95

Blending Sounds into Words

oysters

slime

wrist

dinner

seafood

Mastery Test

Lessons 91–95

Letter-Sound Correspondences

igh

ay

au

ew

ph

wr

kn

Lessons 91-95

Mastery Test

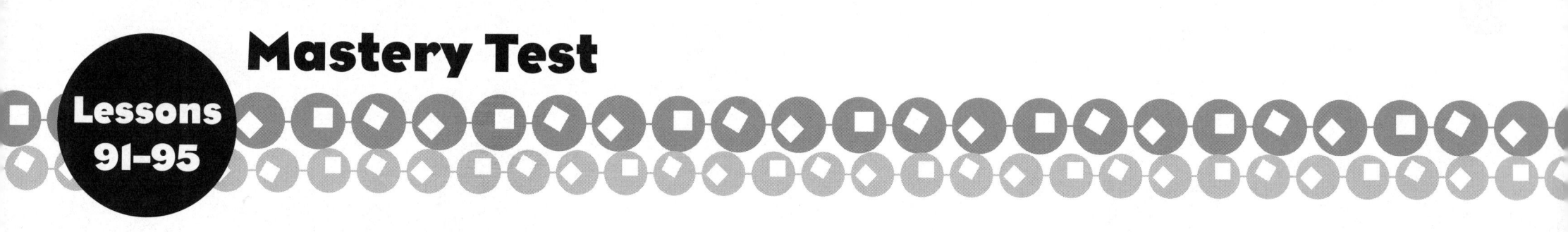

Blending Sounds into Words

knot

wrecker

graph

grew

cause

tray

sigh

Mastery Test

Lessons 91–95

Sentence Reading

Phillis knew that poor Lew had hurt his wrist when he fell off the new seesaw.

Lesson 96

Letter-Sound Correspondences

ace wr ph

ew kn

Letter-Sound Correspondences

mended stumped

rested yelled

stacked planted

Lesson 96

Blending Sounds into Words

face

eyes

ears

tock

fingers

Lesson 96

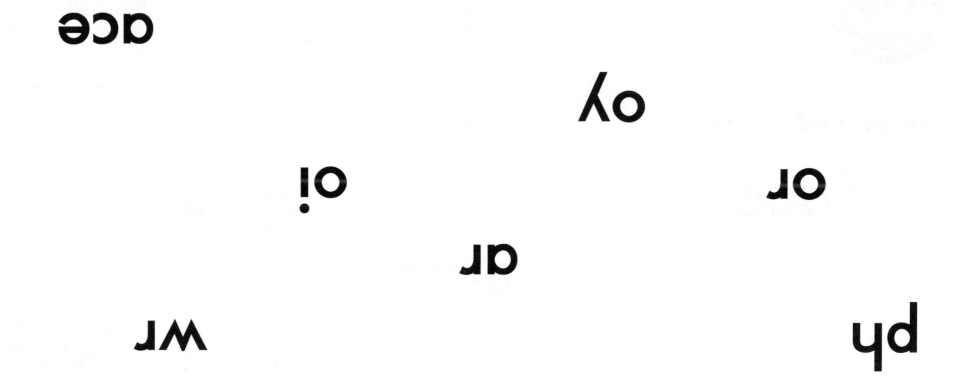

Review: Letter-Sound Correspondences

ph

wr

ar

or

oi

oy

ace

Lesson 96

Review: Blending Sounds into Words

trace

Boyd

coil

scorch

chart

write

Phillip

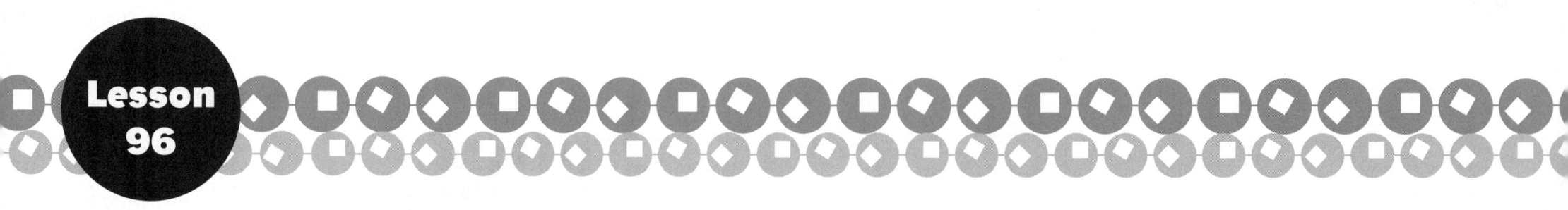

Review: Sentence Reading

Carmen dressed in lace for the talent show.

Lesson 97

Letter-Sound Correspondences

ice

wr

ace

kn

ph

ew

Lesson 97

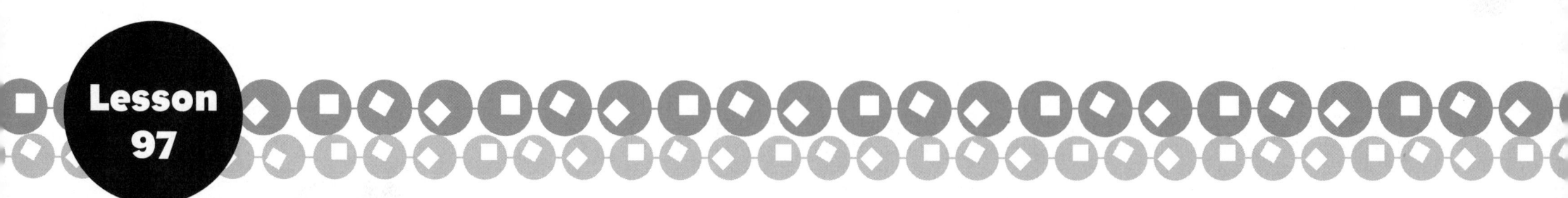

Letter-Sound Correspondences

darted

crawled

pointed

cracked

crashed

shouted

Blending Sounds into Words

ears

white

kernels

garden

popped

Lesson 97

Review: Letter-Sound Correspondences

ace igh ay

au kn

Blending Sounds into Words

space stray

flight

Paul know

Lesson 97

Review: Sentence Reading

Grace might spend nights at Camp Knot for a while.

Lesson 98

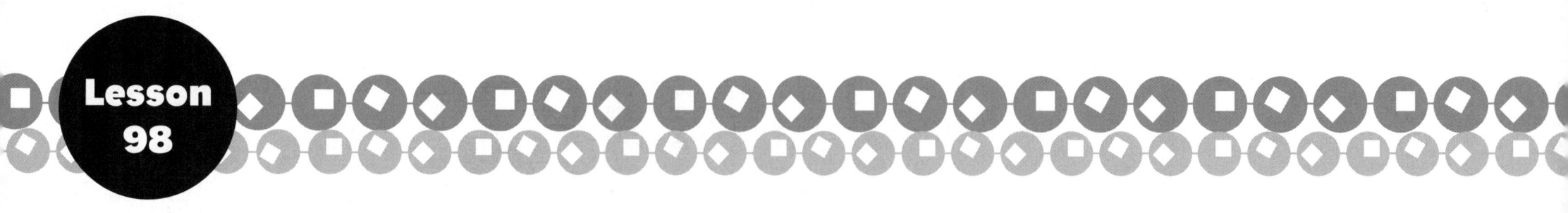

Letter-Sound Correspondences

kn

ew

ph

ace

wr

ice

Blending Sounds into Words

fingers

numbers

close

contact

Lesson 98

Review: Letter-Sound Correspondences

ice

ace

ew

ay

oi

Review: Blending Sounds into Words

twice

place

stew

tray

joining

Lesson 98

Review: Sentence Reading

The rice on my plate was so hot I felt steam on my face.

Lesson 99

Letter-Sound Correspondences

kn

ew

ph

age

ace

wr

ice

Lesson 99

Blending Sounds into Words

goat

horn

finished

round

windows

Lesson 99

Review: Letter-Sound Correspondences

ice ace

ew igh au

Review: Blending Sounds into Words

nice grew

Grace

slight fraud

Lesson 99

Review: Sentence Reading

The mice at the zoo were playing in the maze.

Letter-Sound Correspondences

age ph ice

wr ace

Blending Sounds into Words

spine shelf

tail

found tale

Lessons 96-100

Mastery Test

Letter-Sound Correspondences

ice wr ace

ph kn ew

Blending Sounds into Words

spice wrist race

played Phil knock

chewing

Mastery Test

Sentence Reading

Grace said that we will eat
ice cream twice and go to
a car race when we visit her
nephew Phil.

Lesson 101

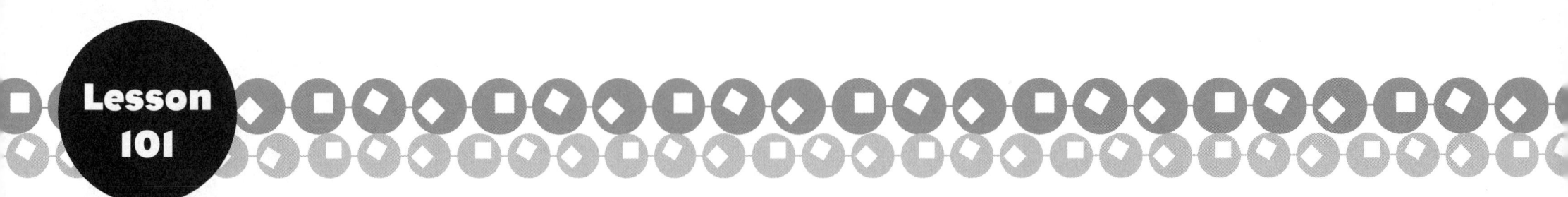

Letter-Sound Correspondences

dge age ice

wr kn ace

ph ew

Blending Sounds into Words

few grade

perform wanted

Lesson 101

Review: Letter-Sound Correspondences

ew

ice

ace

age

Review: Blending Sounds into Words

rage

place

twice

Lew

Lesson 101

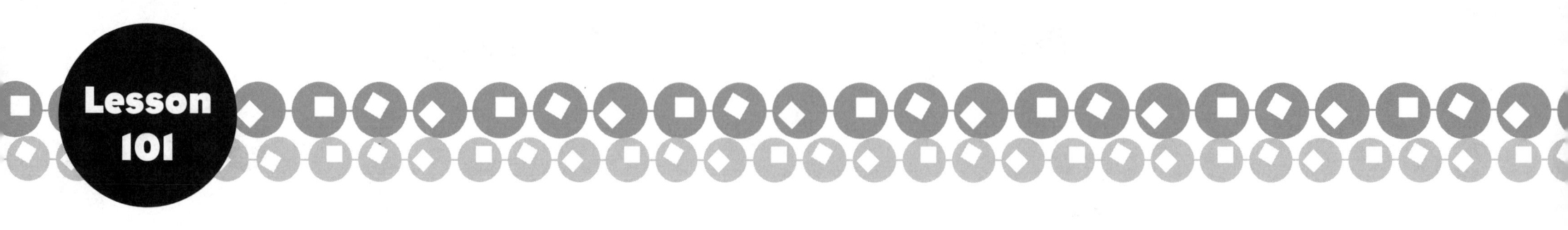

Review: Sentence Reading

We camped at a place near Lew's called Brice Park.

Lesson 102

Letter-Sound Correspondences

dge age

ice wr

ace ph ew kn

Blending Sounds into Words

mice rabbit

twice fawn

Lesson 102

Review: Letter-Sound Correspondences

ace

ice

wr

age

Review: Blending Sounds into Words

wage

price

wrong

race

Review: Sentence Reading

I have won the short race twice, but I lost the long one.

Lesson 103

Letter-Sound Correspondences

tion sion

dge

age ice

wr ace

ph ew kn

Blending Sounds into Words

harness

reader

fantastic

started

acting

Lesson 103

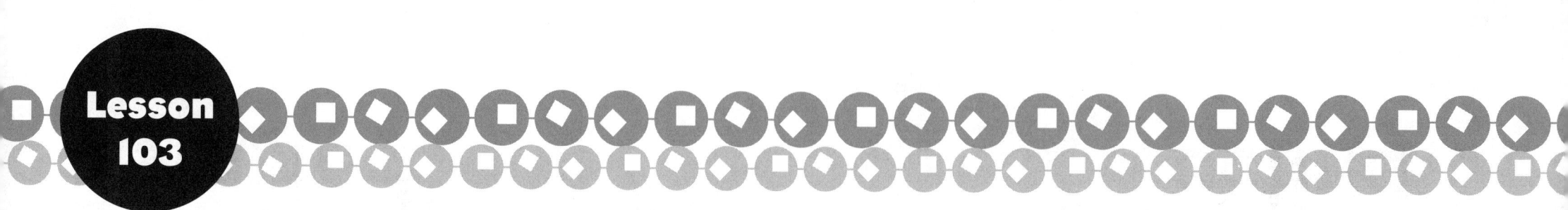

Review: Letter-Sound Correspondences

dge

ice

age

ace

Review: Blending Sounds into Words

edge

stage

slice

trace

Review: Sentence Reading

The mice jumped off the floor onto the stack of hay in the barn.

Lesson 104

Letter-Sound Correspondences

tion dge

age

ice sion

wr

ace

Lesson
104

Blending Sounds into Words

cheerful

stage

race

win

Lesson 104

Review: Letter-Sound Correspondences

dge

sion

tion

Review: Blending Sounds into Words

mōtion

vision

badge

Review: Sentence Reading

The bridge was twice as high as the highest ledge.

Lesson 105

Letter-Sound Correspondences

ong

ice

tion

dge

age

wr

sion

ace

Blending Sounds into Words

action

space

mission

option

Mastery Test

Lessons 101-105

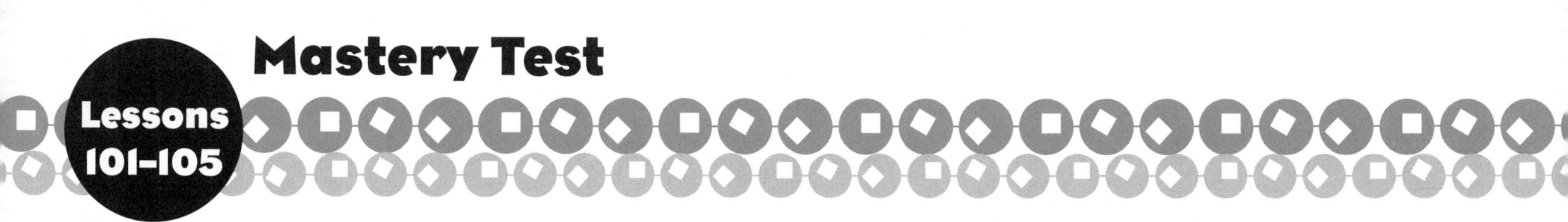

Letter-Sound Correspondences

ace

wr

ice

age

dge

sion

tion

Mastery Test

Lessons 101-105

Blending Sounds into Words

junction mission

trudge

rate handed slice

wrist

face parted

Lessons 101-105

Mastery Test

Sentence Reading

There was a lot of action on the edge of the bridge by the track.

Lesson 106

Letter-Sound Correspondences

ong

tion

sion

dge

age

ice

wr

ace

Lesson 106

Blending Sounds into Words

Madge

summer

Drew

Hodge

Lesson 106

Review: Letter-Sound Correspondences

ice

tion

age

dge

sion

Review: Blending Sounds into Words

fraction

mission

hedge

cage

rice

Lesson 106

Review: Sentence Reading

If I had to guess, I would say that the judge was my mom's age.

Letter-Sound Correspondences

ung

ong

tion

dge

age

ice

sion

ace

Lesson 107

Blending Sounds into Words

peanut

butter

fudge

great

thanks

Lesson 107

Review: Letter-Sound Correspondences

ung

ong

tion

dge

sion

Review: Blending Sounds into Words

wedge

stung

caption

session

fridge

Lesson 107

Review: Sentence Reading

It is my mission to set the plant on the edge of the ledge.

Letter-Sound Correspondences

ace

ung

ice

ong

tion

age

dge

sion

Lesson 108

Blending Sounds into Words

chicken

picnic

blanket

tea

Lesson 108

Review: Letter-Sound Correspondences

ace

ice

ong

ung

Review: Blending Sounds into Words

stung

gong

nice

trace

Review: Sentence Reading

He had a hard time putting his boot on the top rung of the ladder.

Letter-Sound Correspondences

ace

ice

age

dge

sion

tion

ong

ung

Lesson 109

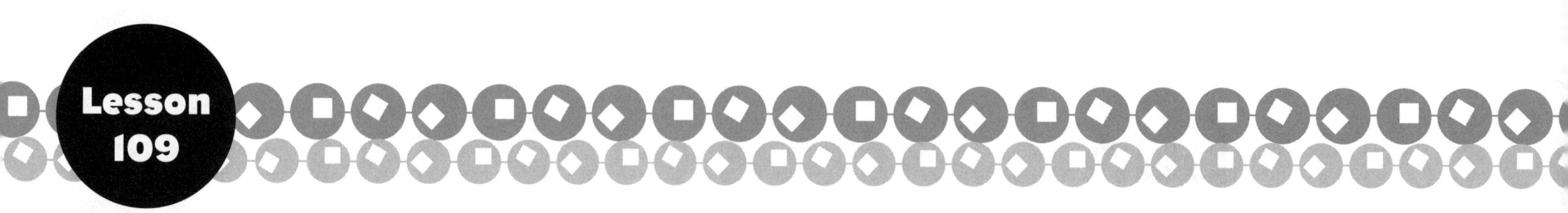

Blending Sounds into Words

blooms

counter

vase

trudge

grassland

Lesson 109

Review: Letter-Sound Correspondences

ong

ung

ace

ice

Review: Blending Sounds into Words

prong

lung

Grace

Brice

Lesson 109

Review: Sentence Reading

The bee stung me twice on my face near my chin.

Letter-Sound Correspondences

ang

ung

ong

ace

tion

dge

sion

age

ice

Lesson 110

Blending Sounds into Words

dodge

picnic

fudge

forms

Mastery Test

Lessons 106–110

Letter-Sound Correspondences

ace ice

age dge

sion ong

ung

tion

Lessons 106–110

Mastery Test

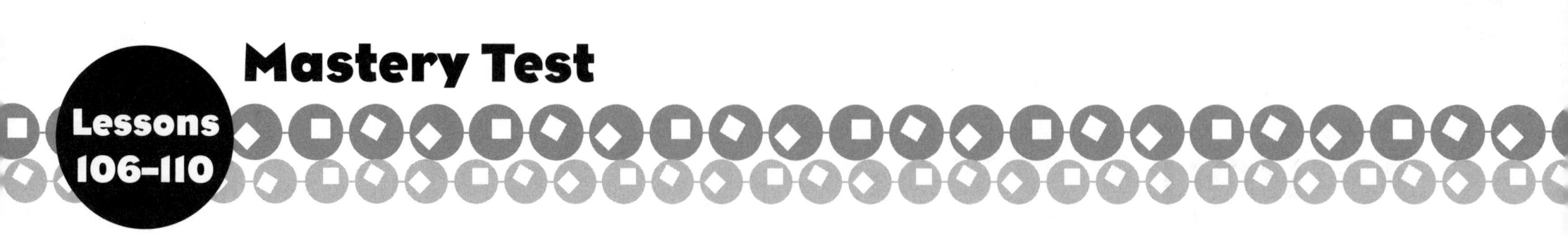

Blending Sounds into Words

strung

strong

action

vision

edge

cage

rice

race

Mastery Test

Sentence Reading

The car slid on the slick ice on the edge of the bridge.